SPIRITUAL CLASSICS

Series Editor: JOHN GRIFFITHS

This series introduces the general reader to works from the various Christian traditions of spirituality which are of enduring value and interest but not generally accessible. It will include some well-known works which will gain a new lease of life from a fresh translation or adaptation, but the emphasis will be on texts not available in any modern English version.

All the works chosen have more than historical interest. They can speak to men and women of today in ways that will often be unexpected, often challenging, never dull. The introduction to each text helps bring the past to life by setting the author (where known) and the work in their cultural, social and historical context, and relating them to streams of thought and belief that, often unconsciously, still influence our beliefs and behaviour today.

The translations and adaptations are responsibly made from the best manuscripts and existing editions, with the prime concern being to present spiritual treasures from past ages in good, direct modern English. Period charm may on occasions be a consideration, but is never allowed to override contemporary effectiveness. The author's message is given precedence without destroying the meaning of the text.

Stripped of difficult and alienating linguistic quirks – of their own time and of other versions, most of them made in the eighteenth or nineteenth centuries – these works show a continuity of vision that makes them contemporary. In this form, they are not of yesterday, but of their time and ours.

A Letter from
Jesus Christ

A LETTER FROM JESUS CHRIST

to the soul that really loves him

by
John of Landsberg

CROSSROAD · NEW YORK

1981
The Crossroad Publishing Company
575 Lexington Avenue, New York, NY 10022

Edited, translated and adapted by John Griffiths
Translation and Introduction Copyright © 1981 by John Griffiths

Library of Congress Catalog Card Number: 81–65449

ISBN: 0–8245–0080–6

Designed and produced by Process Workshop Ltd, London
Photoset by Keyspools Ltd, Warrington
Printed in Great Britain by Billing & Sons Ltd

Contents

A Note on the Illustrations

The illustrations are all reproductions of woodcuts by Albrecht Dürer.

Introduction

In the early sixteenth century Cologne was revered as the Rome of the German lands, a city of saints, scholars, churches and other ecclesiastical institutions. Among them was the Charterhouse of St Barbara, with Joannes Justus Lanspergius, or John (Gerecht) of Landsberg (1489–1539), theologian and mystic, as its prior. John maintained the Carthusian house at a level of spiritual production by then uncommon. He published the first printed editions of the works of St Gertrude, and a large number of ascetical and controversial works of his own which may be seen as linking the militant spirituality of Gertrude with that of the high Counter-Reformation.

He wrote in Latin, but so directly and affectively that his works became extremely popular spiritual manuals and were translated into a number of vernaculars. The major titles are: *Pharetra divino amoris* (Quiver of divine love, Cologne, 1532), *Enchiridion militiae christianae* (Manual of the Christian militia, Cologne, 1538) and *Alloquia Jesus Christi ad fidelem animam* (Address of Jesus Christ to the faithful soul, Cologne, 1555) – which last text proved so simple yet comprehensive a treatise of the Christian life that a hundred years later the little

Jansenist girls at Port Royal were taught from it by Jacqueline Pascal.

Cologne, of course, was also a major city of the Rhineland, an area whose most famous contribution to spirituality was the highly-metaphysical yet lyrically emotive 'Rhineland mysticism' of Eckhart, Tauler and others. John of Landsberg's spirituality shunned both the heights of the metaphysical ascent and the depiction of the profound recesses of the soul where dwelled the inward Lord; he concentrated instead on 'main-line' spirituality and 'practical' issues of the devotional life for as wide and informed an audience as possible. John has been seen as reviving earlier instances of devotion to the heart of God and, through exploitation of the physical imagery of Jesus' passion (his wounds, blood and so on), as anticipating not only the erotic imagery of the religious poets of the Baroque (such as the English Catholic, Richard Crashaw) but later, highly-schematized devotion to the Sacred Heart of Jesus.

Though John's works were not necessarily address-ed initially to lay people, their instructional basis and the careful repetition of key-points show his concern to teach as well as to move; to show concerned Christians where their duties lay. In this he again anticipated interests of the Counter-Reformation of approximately a hundred years later, which recent historians have seen as arising not so much from a desire to counteract the Protestant Reformation as from a realization, shared with the Reformers, that Europe had to be christianized, that paganism was probably the real foe, and that Christian people, clergy, religious and militant lay men and women, had to be taught the main lines of the Christian faith and the Christian life if the masses were to be won over.

At the same time John is teaching a late version of the *devotio moderna*, or new devotion, inspired by van Ruysbroeck and the so-called Brothers of the Common Life. This was Christ-centred, personal, and laid great stress on meditation, but meditation of a structured rather than open-ended kind. Here liturgical practice does not receive such considerable attention as individual devotion to Jesus, but the perennial mystical themes of self-renunciation and self-forgetting, the inward acknowledgement of the cross and suffering, are represented.

*   *   *

John was not a Rhinelander by origin. He was born at Landsberg, Bavaria, in southern Germany, but studied in Cologne and became a professed Carthusian when he was twenty-one. He reports himself as volunteering to wash the brothers' clothes several times a week, in addition to working as a copyist – an example of the practical instances of charity for God's sake which he recommends in his manuals. He also tells us in his autobiographical fragments that early on in his life at the Charterhouse he became interested in summarizing methods of getting rid of vices and replacing them with virtues – methods which he came across in reading or discourse. His schematized notes were at first for his own use but later (as he tells us in the humble phrase used by so many authors over the centuries), 'persuaded by friends', he agreed to write up the lot for book publication (as the *Enchiridion*).

After ten years he became a master of novices, a demanding duty which required even more structuring of the lessons won from his notes and from personal meditation and practice, largely in silence. This didactic concern was increased by the contemporary progress of the Reformation, which accounts for the very precise underlining of the Catholic notion of 'faith and works' in John's writings.

John became a prior in 1530 when he moved to the Charterhouse of the Sorrows of Our Lady at Vogelsang, to the west of Cologne. He also acted as official preacher to the Duke of Jülich, in the same area, and later published the many sermons that he delivered. He also wrote *A Letter from Jesus Christ* for an abbey of Premonstratensian nuns. After four years he was released from his office as prior because of bad health and returned to the Charterhouse of St Barbara. Two years later he was appointed vicar there. He died three years afterwards.

The *Letter* proved to be one of his most widely-read works. It appeared in his lifetime in a collective volume and separately after his death, and was translated first into Spanish in the late sixteenth century, then into French in the mid-seventeenth century. One of the best-known translations for some three hundred years was the English version of Blessed Philip Howard, the nineteenth Earl of Arundel, and son of the fourth Duke of Norfolk.

*　　*　　*

Philip Howard was born in 1557, and therefore during the reign of Mary Tudor. He was brought up as a Catholic in infancy but later by Protestants, and went to Cambridge in its very Protestant years. He came down when he was eighteen. His father had been executed for treason when Philip was fifteen and though he succeeded his uncle as Earl of Arundel in 1581, and he was one of her favourites, Elizabeth never made him Duke of Norfolk. He would not seem to have been interested in matters religious until he attended an enforced disputation between the imprisoned Jesuit, Edmund Campion, some other priests and some Anglicans. Almost a year later his wife Anna was secretly reconciled to Catholicism. The Queen discovered the fact, and Philip was soon confined under house arrest, following his wife into the Roman Church in 1584. The next year he tried to escape to continental Europe but government agents caught up with him before he landed. He was charged with plotting together with Mary, Queen of Scots, and sent to the Tower of London. He was sentenced to death in 1589 for having Mass said for the Spanish Armada, but the sentence was suspended while he continued in imprisonment. He died in 1595 after eleven years in the Tower. While there, he wrote devotional verse (one hymn – a translation from John of Landsberg – appears at the end of the present book) and translated spiritual works, among which was *The Epistle of Jesus Christ to the Faithful Soul*, which became a favourite devotional manual of English Catholics into this century. The first edition appeared before 1595 but no copy survives. The second edition was printed in 1595 at Antwerp or possibly (as with many rescusant books that concealed their origin with a false place of publication) in England. It was entitled: 'An Epistle in the Person of Christ to the faithful soul. Written first by that learned Lanspergius, and after translated into English by one of no small fame, whose good example of sufferance and living hath and will be a memorial unto his country and posterity for ever'. The third edition appeared in 1610 without a place of publication and was entitled: 'An Epistle or Exhortation of Jesus Christ to the soul, that is devoutly affected towards him. Wherein are contained certain divine inspirations, teaching a man to know himself, and instructing him in the perfection of true piety. Written in Latin by the devout servant of Christ, Joannes Lanspergius, a Charterhouse Monk. And translated into English by the Lord Philip, late Earl of Arundel. *Permissu Superiorum* M.D.C.X.' It was dedicated to the English Poor Clares at Gravelines and the dedication was signed with the initials of John Wilson, who had a press at St Omer's English College. The dedication is an interesting summary of the book's nature and of the ends to which it was applied in its first English translation: 'To the Reverend Mother and Devout Poor Sisters of the holy Order of S. Clare in the first English Convent erected in Graveling. This brief but most excellent Epistle of *Jesus Christ to the Faithful Soul*: (Religious Poor Sisters) worthy, no doubt, both of the Author's piety and Translator's virtue, being so much by you and others desired, and now the third time printed, I have thought it both to your profit and for your consolation to present the same unto you, as a mirror or looking-glass, who, being now entered into the path of Virtue, do earnestly endeavour to arrive to the height of Christian Religious Perfection; especially at this time, when almost all virtuous life and devotion in our Country, by the unfortunate sway of Schism and Heresy, lieth, as it were, languishing and sick even unto death itself, that by this means some little sparks of piety may be conserved alive within the embers of your religious hearts, not only of those who, by your virtuous example, shall follow your footsteps, but of others also into whose hands this Golden Treatise, so particularly due unto yourselves for the rare documents of perfection it containeth shall happily come. Our sweet Saviour increase daily your earnest desire of religious Piety, and preserve you ever. Amen. Your servant in Christ Jesus, I.W. PRIEST".

There were two reprints in the nineteenth century and one in the early twentieth century.

* * *

The present version of the book is made from Philip Howard's time-honoured translation, with reference to the original. It has been freely adapted for the modern reader. John of Landsberg was intent on ramming home important points of disputed doctrine and used the device of summary repetition in a way acceptable to the readers of centuries past when persecution and sharp religious divisions made such manuals precious. Nowadays judicious excisions do not harm but bring out the directness of the book's message. Its appealing mixture of lyricism, sudden vivid similes, neat inclusion of quotations from the Bible, and reinforcement of the picture of the soul centred on Jesus Christ, are of course preserved.

The book's most engaging device is its presentation as a letter from Jesus himself. This retains its shock-value, and the author's not wholly disingenuous remarks (considering possible contemporary re-actions) about the authorship in his preface to the Premonstratensian nuns, do not reduce the effect. Apart from the echoes of the *devotio moderna*, and the somewhat strict recommendations that we associate with the *Imitation of Christ*, the other central device is

16

that of 'bridal mysticism' in the shape of the traditional presentation of Jesus as the soul's lover and the soul as his faithful spouse. This aspect is emphasized and at times reaches the level of a domesticized eroticism that is intentional but hardly as extreme as some of the metaphors of the Spanish mystics or even the great original of the Song of Songs. The figure of the soul as a dutiful wife also follows faithfully the contemporary notion of a woman's subservience to her husband – a concept that has to remain, for if it were removed entirely the book's essential structure would be damaged. It is outweighed, however, by the stress on the reciprocal love between the soul and Christ; with due attention to the imbalance of the relationship, but with constant reference to the goodness of God who in spite of his utter otherness so loves the human individual that it is as if he depended on an equal ardour in his soul-bride.

Firmly, however, John reminds us that God is the only source of the soul's ability to love and that he requires to be loved for himself alone. There is a corresponding insistence, too, on the human form divine, on the importance of good works and love of one's neighbour, that strikes an especially modern note. This is amplified by the many remarks, ranging from questions of diet to problems of leading a reserved devotional life in the company of other people, that show the author's long acquaintance with the realities of community life.

There are no traces of the quietism and sometimes near-approval of inaction that caused such seventeenth-century spiritual manuals as those of Molinos and Fénélon to be condemned for neglect both of the notion of salvation and of the spiritual person's duties in the world. John preserves the cardinal mystical ideas of the spiritual marriage, refusal of self and of liking for outward things, and a stress on the individual's nothingness before God, but he does not venture into the realm of the Rhineland mystics, Teresa of Avila and John of the Cross, in which the soul intent on the Godhead must cross the barrier of its natural abilities and embark on a voyage beyond the end of the night. The way marked out here, though one for those who seek to be out of the world while transitory beings in it, is not for the exceptional contemplative but for the 'ordinary' devout. Sighs and even the fire of love are required, yet prudence is not only recommended but enjoined on the basis of precise reminders of human infirmity both inward and outward. For all its echoes of a harsher and therefore stricter age, and one in which a high price was often exacted in external life for a socially inappropriate choice of doctrine or practice, the *Letter* displays a leniency and tenderness, and understanding of human restrictions and constrictions, which probably would not have seemed apt to adult rather than infant Jansenists.

John also inserts (judiciously, again, for there must

be no imbalance between the affective and instructive elements of the work) poignant graphic passages which look back to the religious imagery of suffering humanity in the late Middle Ages (to, say, Grünewald's Isenheim altarpiece of the degraded Christ), and which must have been singularly relevant to Philip Howard sentenced without trial and cutting a crucifix into his cell wall in the Beauchamp Tower: 'When I stand knocking at your door I shall be very weak and shivering with cold and need you very much. When I stand at your door I shall be as I was when they freed me from the pillar they bound me to, to whip me and wound me for your sake. When I show myself to you I show myself in the form of a man weak, degraded and insulted. I want to impress my image on your mind as one suffering and wounded, so that you take pity on me and lift me up and embrace me, and hold me with the arms of your love'. Or: 'I was born in a stable near the mouths of animals, the heat of whose breath was my defence against the bitter cold. I was laid upon hay in a manger. I was saved by the sacrifice of poor innocents. When I was an infant I was driven into banishment'. Clearly these images have not lost their relevance in our own age of unspeakable tortures and disregard of the love of justice which John says should be the faithful Christian's concern.

His picture of the Church, too, has an unmistakably modern ring. It is biblical, of course, and impeccably orthodox, but in the extended simile of Christians as members of the Body of Christ, each with his or her own talents, contributing to one mysteriously effective whole, it strikes a communitarian note that brings the *Letter*, for all its now unappealing references to the lowliness and abjectness of the individual, to obedience, and to the dangers of natural desires and personal impulses, into line with our own not so original emphases on the Church as community: 'Whatever this body has in one limb should be used to the benefit of the rest. Every member of my body ought to make one another a sharer in the gifts which every one of them receives, because of the union of the body and the communion of love which exists among them ... You have nothing that is your own. What do you possess that you have not received? ... You have nothing that is given to you alone, that is, you have nothing that is given to you for yourself alone, but everything that you have received is committed to your care to be used entirely for the benefit of the whole body of my Church'. There is nothing here, and nothing indeed in the book as a whole, which is absolutely irrelevant to any branch of the Church in our times. The polemical note of the *Letter* has disappeared like so much dust between the fingers, and it is hoped that in this new version this unpretentious and moving work will speak across boundaries that at one time it could not cross.

John Griffiths

THE AUTHOR'S LETTER

To the Venerable Mother and religious virgins of the Premonstratensian Order, dedicated to Christ in the Monastery of Hensberch, John of Landsberg, Prior of the Carthusians, wishes grace and peace.

I am sure that all you devout virgins will agree with me that no one could be so ignorant as to suppose that the following speech or exhortation, which is ascribed to our blessed Saviour Jesus Christ, was something that he spoke with his own mouth, or actually gave out in any sort of way when he lived on this earth. It is pretty obvious that I've given it this rather splendid title because it contains no more and no less than the teachings which are truly and really Jesus's. That soon becomes clear if you compare it with his actual words, and with what he teaches us in our hearts. What I have done is to write down what Christ tells us and we feel he tells us, inside us, in our hearts, as if he were talking or writing to us straightforwardly.

The nature of the human mind is such that it is much more prepared to listen, and to do what should be done, if it realizes that no ordinary man or woman but Jesus himself is talking. We are always much more interested in and persuaded by something we hear, if we know that the person speaking is truly wise and has the kind of standing that promises worthwhile advice.

My intention in writing this book was that the spirit of Jesus Christ should shine into the hearts and minds of those who read it and really help them. And so I should like as many people as possible to read it, not for my sake but in the name of Jesus.

As long as we remain mortal creatures, subject to corruption and decay, our minds and souls are most easily moved, stirred up and persuaded to reach out to God, by means of things that we receive through our senses and that our human understanding can easily grasp. That is why the Church uses all kinds of ceremonies and objects in services, such as organs, hymn-singing and so on. Other obvious examples are the images and pictures of Christ and of the saints which ordinary people like to say their prayers in front of. When they look at statues and paintings they remember how good Christ has been to them, or want to follow the good examples they see portrayed before them, or else, focussing their minds and hearts on Jesus himself, offer up their genuine devotion, not to sticks and stones, but to the real person, Jesus himself, whom the artist or craftsman has tried to picture for them. Of course we know very well that the picture of Jesus we see isn't Jesus Christ himself, although when we're very moved or taken up in prayer, it looks as if we were worshipping the image. What we are, or should be doing, is fixing our minds not on the picture but on the person it represents. This letter from Jesus is designed to be read in the same way: not because it was either written or spoken by Jesus himself, just as it is, but as if it were written by him, for I assure you that everything taught or stated in it is exactly what Jesus Christ says every day, but inwardly of course, to the devout soul that loves him and for that reason has long been described as his spouse.

So all you readers who have decided in some way to reject the vanities of this world, read what your lover Jesus has to say to you, remembering that it is no more and no less than what he says all the time in a special and mysterious way in the depths of your own hearts.

A LETTER FROM
JESUS CHRIST
TO THE SOUL
THAT REALLY LOVES HIM

This letter is from Jesus Christ the Saviour of the world and the King of heaven and earth, who is ready to welcome and embrace all those who truly want him, and to hold them in his merciful and fatherly arms. All he wants is that his spouse, the soul which loves him and for whose sake he willingly suffered death so that they might be joined together, should be perfectly and truly happy.

My dear daughter, you know that I love you very much indeed. I have often spoken to you inside your very own heart, but you haven't listened to me. Therefore, since you have never answered me or done what I asked, the great love I feel for you has made me write to you. I hope that at the very least you won't object to reading what you ignored when I spoke to you. Perhaps, when you read what I have to say, it will stay fixed in your mind so that you carry it with you wherever you go.

You see, I love you so much that I not only put myself in all sorts of dangerous situations, but suffered the outcome and even exposed myself to death for your sake. The same love is so strong in me that I can't leave anything undone that might help to save you. Even though you show no sign whatsoever of answering my love with your own, because you're intent on superficial, silly and passing things, and therefore too much taken up with the outward aspects of things I have made, I still can't stop loving you. I love you so much that I'm always ready to take you into my arms. I love you, you see, much more than any father loves his or any mother her children. I'm not only willing to give you everything you really need but I want you as my own spouse. If only you follow my advice I shall give you, day after day, greater and better blessings that you will ever find in this world.

The trouble is that when I visited you inwardly and tried to inspire you, you just wouldn't listen to anything I had to say and got into the habit of blocking your inward ears and eyes to me. You got accustomed to shutting me off and became so very distracted from your own true self that you couldn't even conceive what you had lost or the sad, dull state you're in. Oddly enough, the less you realize the poor condition of your mind and heart, the more you deserve to be pitied.

I suppose the best point to start at is what you should be doing. Should be ... Yes, above all you should be an example to others and your life should help other people who have gone wrong to go right. When you talk, what you say should be so sensible – yet attractively sensible – to those who hear it, that it has the immediate effect of an antibiotic on their weak, tired or sick spirits. Even better, your words should be so powerful that they leap out like flames and fire the heart of anyone listening. In fact, you're so concerned with childish things, and a lot of matters that in the end are no good to anyone, your thoughts wander so much and you're always dreaming of what might be but can't be and isn't important anyway, that nothing you say could spark any enthusiasm in any respect. In short, you're still in love with yourself. Before you can be a joy and inspiration to others and teach them something, you have to learn not to love yourself.

Wherever you are, whatever you do and wherever you go, I am always with you, always watching over you. I see the reality of all your actions and impulses and what you truly intend in the depths of your heart. Because I am utterly loyal to you, the least unfaithfulness to me on your part offends me. I have suffered, quite willingly, insults, reproaches, unhappiness and even torment for your sake.

* * *

I'm not going to describe in detail all the pain and savagery I had to put up with. All I shall do is to ask you: Do you know anyone else who would suffer so much disgrace and rottenness for a friend, as I suffered for you? I endured them when you, to all intents and purposes, were my enemy, when you hadn't done a thing that was any good to anyone; I suffered them too when you neither loved me nor knew me. Before you were born I loved you and suffered anguish and pain for you. Don't turn away from me. Why do you look for peace and satisfaction anywhere but with me? If only you could see how depressed and ill you are, you wouldn't go on rushing about from one thing to another.

Ask yourself: If I left you (but I won't), who in the end would care for you as I do? Can anyone else cure what's really wrong with you? Whatever you look at, whatever you fix your mind on will give you no peace, no joy, no rest, though it may deceive you into thinking now that it will. I am your only peace, joy and rest. Your senses cheat you, and the people who seem to love you are as often abusing you. The extent of your self-deception is such that all the time you are taking doses of a poison which in the end will numb and kill you, and refusing a medicine that will bring you true life.

I know very well how often things which seem beautiful and attractive but are actually useless appeal to you sensually and lead you away by guile and deceit. Remember that you are a spouse and that the only love in your heart should be love of your husband. There is nothing you should desire but his affection for you, to be beautiful for him, to please him and to be his beloved for ever.

I stand here desiring you and waiting for you. I want you to return to me with your whole heart. Leave all these vain and useless things. Become wholly devoted to me, and quite humble in heart, so that I can talk to you more closely and lovingly and please your mind with delights that are far better and far purer than those that have drenched you for so long.

I don't want you to do a whole lot of things, to agonize over this or that exceptional way of pleasing me. I want a chaste, faithful and pure heart which isn't interested in its own pleasures. I want sincere love and fervent devotion. I want a will that is ready and eager to honour me and obey me, and a sincere and pure intention to do what I really want you to do.

I want your heart to be clear and free from any other love whatsoever. If you give me your heart like that, then I shall comfort and console you and bless you more wonderfully than you would ever dare to think, more indeed than ever you could think of.

I am not the forward kind of husband who would approach you when you were busy with other matters of no value whatsoever. When I come to you I must find you alone. When I stand knocking at your door I shall be very weak and shivering with cold and need you very much. When I stand at your door I shall be as I was when they freed me from the pillar they bound me to, to whip me and wound me for your sake. When I show myself to you I show myself in the form of man weak, degraded and insulted. I want to impress my image on your mind as one suffering and wounded, so that you take pity on me and lift me up and embrace me, and hold me with the arms of your love. And then

33

A letter from Jesus Christ

I can unite myself with you and fire your love with the suffering of my love – my love for you.

If only you would recognize me as your husband and love me as you ought to, then you would take me straight into your heart. Even before I came to your door, you would long for me, and wait for however long it seemed before I came to you. Then you would clothe the naked, and bring the cold and lost before your fire, and be worthy to receive my chaste embrace, the sweet taste of my spirit, and my love.

* * *

I am happy if you trust me, surely and firmly; I am happy if you are as willing to be with me as I desire to be with you: for all my pleasure is found in human company. If you trust in me and desire to be with me then every day your strength of mind will increase and your soul grow more sweetly loving. But there is something odd about trusting in me. You can never do so unless you distrust yourself. To trust me and distrust yourself you have to be poor in spirit. And in the real life poverty of spirit is a most precious jewel. But I know very well what stops you from having this virtue. You have too much of a taste for this world. Strangely enough, that makes you so cold that you virtually loathe and resist the word of God, which is the food of your soul. But if you want to increase in virtue and to strengthen your mind by doing what is virtuous, you must not only have a taste for the word

34

of God but gobble it up greedily, swallow it down and digest it perfectly so that it actually becomes a part of you and goes on nourishing you.

The reason why you can't thirst for my justice is that you are already full up with the cold meats of worldly conversation and vanity. You have had so much of them and are so addicted to them that your palate has no taste for piety and devotion. You just can't stand simplicity of heart. Meditation, as far as you are concerned, is a sheer waste of time. Your mind is so taken up with the cares of this world that the weight of them in you drags it down and stops it rising up to me. Even if you force it to ascend for a minute or two, the weight of the world in you pulls it down again into earthly thoughts. Your soul is distracted, your heart is inconstant, your mind wavers, and your desires are caught up in the love of worldly pleasures. And what is the result? You are troubled when awake, and fretful when asleep.

As you know, you're really quite miserable. When you realize how miserable you are, you start to complain, saying you feel dry and empty – 'Jesus, I feel awful, why do you make me feel like this?' But if in fact you were in the kind of empty state that I'm quite prepared to let people be in (it happens to many other friends of mine), and not in a condition due entirely to your own negligence, there would be no reason whatsoever for you to feel that my grace was lacking in you. But, seeing as your own sloth and

35

carelessness are the reason why you lie there languishing in this barren dryness, if you want me to console you, if you wish me to come to you, if you long to be joined to me, then you have to give up all those useless things which please you apart from me. Instead you must do all you can to please me and serve me. You must try continually to do the things that I like best. If you make that your main concern, you will have to use all your force and might to come as close as possible to seeing that everyone else does my will. When you do that, rely on me and on me alone. Then you will sense my presence more and more until you reach the point where your spirit is drunk with joy. Your conscience will be comforted, your heart will be at peace, and you will enter into the perfect rest of sweetest contemplation.

*　　*　　*

If you had only once entered the wine-cellar I'm talking about, you would always be thirsty to be there as often as possible. But the only people who can get into my wine-store are those who desire me more than anything else, love me more than anything else, and know that I am all in all. Anyone who finds consolation only in me, and thinks that he or she is unworthy to receive my comfort, or wants affliction so much in this world that he or she even feels somehow wronged when I send the least consolation, and as willingly accepts my leaving that soul without any comfort as when I fill it with my consolation; anyone to whom all joy without me is a torment, and has his or her mind wholly fixed on me and wants only to serve me; such a person is my special friend at whose door I willingly knock and freely enter. That is the kind of person to whom I gladly offer myself and tell my secrets. That is the kind of person whom I visit in the least expected ways, as seems best to me in each case. For each one there is a special way to stir and inspire the soul that loves me.

Sometimes I show myself to their soul's eyes, wounded, naked and tortured in every limb. So that the love they have for me can be truly comforted, I show them my pain and my suffering, so that they can help me, and bathe my wounds, and kiss my sorrow and embrace me. Even though the devotion shown to me in my suffering human form may seem ridiculous to worldly people (who haven't any idea what it means), it is what I want most of all. When a spouse of mine loves those who are suffering and helps them, then I begin to forget all the pains which I have undergone, and all the faults which my spouse has committed against me, and I do all I can to comfort her with my spirit and to offer the grace which turns all burdens to nothingness.

Strange to say, even though I never need anything, I know that I have gained something very precious when I find that my loved one is so faithful that she loves me more than herself or all the world besides.

But ungratefulness offends me as much as loyalty contents me. It hurts me more than anything, because thanklessness is as if someone were trying with all his or her strength to open all my old wounds – all the sorrow of my passion and all the mental suffering I went through. I am hurt because it is as if everything I suffered out of love were like dust.

So, whether you suffer physical pain in your body or mental pain in your mind, don't try to compensate it with some mundane substitute. In all your distress of body or mind, rush and look for me. Don't start complaining or wailing to any person, but just tell me everything that worries you. The greatest help that any human being can give you is in the end no more than well-chosen words and well-turned phrases. You know that. Of course, if you know a priest or pastor who would be of help, you must go to him and explain the secret things in your heart that are troubling you, then follow his advice – but without giving in, in any way, to the kind of satisfaction that comes from pouring it all out angrily, or pushing to get some superficial consolation, or boasting to others about the ghastly things you have to put up with.

Tell me in secret what you're longing to complain about to all and sundry. Put yourself and everything to do with you in my hands, and try to simmer down. Shut out all the vexation and worry and perturbation by giving it to me. If you do that you will find a happy peace coming over you – even though it won't always be the kind of peace that you imagine or would like or dream of, but what is right for you.

* * *

On the other hand, it won't do you any harm, but help you to keep a cool head in all adversities, if you remember the story of my life, the things I did and the miseries I went through, even picturing them as best you can. There is no better way to make all bitter things sweet. If you meditate like that, and suffer with me, you will find that the rival images of your own worries are banished from your mind. Leave your outward world for the inward realm of your own self and hear me cry in your heart. Hear my sorrow and see the bitterness of my days: 'My God, my God why have you left me?' If you think like that, then you will want to imitate me, to suffer for me, and to serve me without any comfort at all, forgetting yourself altogether.

Those who serve me in that frame of mind, who are united with me out of love alone, and stay faithful to me only to please me, and so that my will can be done through them, those are my most faithful and most special friends. Whatever dryness and desolation they seem to be in, and whatever temptations appear to overwhelm them (even if it seems that I have cast them off and abandoned them), they are still truly mine, because they go on struggling against the temptations that always attack people in the war of this world, and never leave my side even though sometimes it seems to them that I am striking them down and punishing them.

I never leave them. They have conquered their passions and curbed their appetites to please me. Because they have abandoned their own selves and given themselves to me alone, and are subject to my will, why, I can't stop myself but have to pour myself into them so that I fill, nourish and possess their souls with my comfort, which is a hundred times better, purer and sweeter than the worldly pleasure which they have given up. But (as I have often told you and will go on insisting so that you can't say you didn't know it), those who run after and accept some alien consolation that has nothing to do with me, and isn't in me at all, cannot receive my own sweet comfort. My consolation is so sweet that you can taste its pure sweetness only if you allow no tawdry saccharine taste into your mouth. It is so pure that it cannot be mixed with any consolation that comes from the things I have made. – But why do I repeat all this so often? – To make you wiser, more watchful and more careful, and so that you do not forget me for false pleasures. You can forget me but I can never forget you, even though your salvation depends entirely on me, and not mine on you in any way at all.

I also want you to be with me always, and by being with me to be happy. Then why, you ask, don't I plunge you directly into eternal bliss? For your own good, so that hour by hour you may grow in virtue and learn how precious a jewel time is, and say: 'Jesus who loves me has given me this hour and this moment, and has prolonged my life this far, so that I can turn to him'.

*   *   *

Stop a minute! Just think: The present moment, this very minute of your existence, is the first of your life in which you really do right, and see everything you have done in the past as nothing. Use every occasion, every event, all work and all leisure, and everything that could or will happen to you, to benefit your soul and serve my purpose. When I stir you up and excite and inspire your spirit so that you abandon everything vain and pointless, and then slam the doors of your senses on all mundane things, it is so that you can return to me with a quiet mind.

*   *   *

Now that you are (as I trust) in a receptive state, recollected and peaceful, and ashamed of all your errors and omissions, I can describe the plain path which will never take you away from me.

I

A rule for a spiritual life

I hope you will now listen very attentively to what I have to say. Anyway, you give every sign of wanting to do so, and so I shall tell you what I expect you to do now that you have come back to me. If there is anything that you think you cannot do of yourself, let prayer help you.

You should pray to try to get whatever you really need. Say: 'Save me from my enemies, Lord. Lord, I fly to you for help. Teach me to do your will, for you are my God. Do not leave me, Lord God; and do not despise me, for you are the God of my salvation. Help me, Lord, for you are the God of my safety. I want to come back to you, so take me with you and never let me be separated or withdrawn from you again'.

Remember and keep in your heart what I told one of my servants long ago. Try to go beyond keeping it in your heart – actually do it:

> Use ever silence in your tongue,
> And have compunction in your mind;
> Be humble, courteous, meek and mild,
> If you in me will comfort find.

I want you to do all you can to be sorry for your sins.

I want you to forget all other concerns and to focus your mind on a continual, internal conversation. Stay away from all other pleasures and retire into your own soul, shutting out any distraction or worry whatsoever. Be absolutely silent and scour your heart until it is quite clean and pure. Be humble and meek, and remember to be courteous and gentle towards all kinds of people.

*   *   *

First of all, examine yourself very carefully indeed. Look very closely and in great detail into your very own self, so that you are well aware of every little thing in you that stops my grace. Look for everything that could displease me so that you can correct and amend it. Think of things and ways that tempt you and try in your heart to resist them with all your might. Where you find you're really weak, be more forceful and quickly expel the temptation. Think of all the occasions which you know make you sin, or prevent you from profiting from a spiritual way of life, and simply cut yourself off from them.

Take special care to show me a pure heart. By that I mean not only what is obvious, that it should be free from all uncleanness, and without any improper love for anyone or anything I have made, but that you should not occupy yourself with anything in this world that is unnecessary. Try with all your force of self to keep close to me and always to rely on me. I want you to make this a continual practice so that you can keep yourself free from any alien or wandering thoughts. You can never do that unless you lead an internal and solitary life, a private life in your very own self, withdrawn from all worldly concerns.

Many people complain that they are not suited to contemplation and the spiritual life when the real reason is their own negligence and laziness. 'I'm just not that sort of person', they say, when in fact they don't want to make an effort to change themselves and subdue their ordinary and secret longings but instead rather like feeding them, even cherishing them and working hard to make them flourish, when they really ought to be not just pruning but digging them up by the roots and casting them out of mind. They walk about with a heavy load of restless thoughts, spending a lot of time and trouble on them. Banish all pointless talk, silly cares and any kind of business that doesn't benefit your soul. Never set your mind to work on anything or trouble yourself with anything that doesn't help my cause, save your soul, or do your neighbour good. Then you will find that you are collected and recollected in yourself, and happily alone with me, whom no other companion or occupation can match.

2

Squashing pointless and wrong desires and inclinations

Don't listen to, much less read, any news, gossip or silly anecdotes which might affect your clear and balanced judgment of self and delight only a wayward mind, leaving your soul, once delighted, to dream of vain desires and flit from one quaint mind-picture to another. Avoid all special familiarity with, affection for and gossip with worldly people who love only earthly pleasures.

Make sure that you control your belly so that you feed it with no more than it needs. Don't eat to delight your palate but to stay alive. Eat for my sake, which means not letting your body or mind decay but becoming more able to serve me. Never please your tongue with things that are unnecessary and harm your body – though of course you must not offend people by refusing things merely in order to appear virtuous. Avoid things which you eat or drink for pleasure beyond necessity, things which any of your body's sweet teeth crave for. But be discreet: charity comes before extremity. Don't make yourself ill and don't do anything unnatural. Self-control doesn't mean anorexia.

Yes, I know, some things are necessary and yet you can't have them without some kind of pleasure. Well and good. All you have to do is not seek for the delightful aspect as it were apart from me. In other words, I have committed your body to you to look after. Eat, drink and so on as required, and accept the pleasure, but do not indulge yourself for pleasure's sake. Watch over your senses so that they don't move off so to speak on their own. See nothing, touch nothing, know nothing, but what profits your soul and honours me.

Pleasing your own fancy by following your appetite for appetite's sake, because you feel like it, because the desire suddenly comes over you – that is offensive, whether in food and drink, or in any other natural process, even in seeking the sheer pleasure of a spiritual consolation. Pleasure for its own sake drives and separates you clean from me. So don't nurture any longing, and don't use your body just for your liking or to please your own will, even when it seems to be a 'good' thing. As I said, even religious practices can be misused in this way. You must shut out all love of yourself and all desire to follow your own appetite. Let pure and simple charity (without any admixture of any other thing whatsoever), and a chaste intention to please me, stir and move you to every single thought you think, to every single word you utter, and to every single action you engage in.

3
Checking your tongue

Be as wary as possible about everything you say. Setting the tongue at liberty is not a work of charity. Let it say nothing but what is necessary and what you have considered carefully in advance. Use as few words as possible to express what you have to say. Be modest and humble when you speak. No great noise, no loud words. Avoid by every means possible any occasion that tempts you speak to no purpose. Stop short as soon as you realize that your mouth has run away with you.

Never say anything that is in any way hurtful, backbiting or grudging, unclean or argumentative; shun it as you would a mortal sin. Use every means in your power to avoid empty talk, laughter for laughter's sake, and all idle words, whether they come from your own mind or are prompted by someone else.

In order to avoid the great vice of backbiting, decide firmly in your own heart never to say a word about anyone who isn't present when you say it, unless you are absolutely sure that what you have to say will do people good. The safest rule, as soon as anyone starts talking about people behind their back, is to have some ploy ready to cut it off – quickly talk about something else, breaking in straightaway before criticism or slander hits the air.

Be very, very careful not to speak yourself or to allow anyone else to speak of people who have offended you in some way, or of those about whom you don't feel perfectly charitable in your heart. That is one of the easiest ways to fall into the vice of backbiting – you are often ready to hear people who know exactly how to please you by flattering you and then criticizing others they are well aware you can't stand. So be especially on your guard against accusations made against your enemies or people you don't like.

*   *   *

Try your best to stay silent most of the time. I'm thinking not merely of the silence of your tongue, but above all of the silence of your heart. Be silent within so that you can't hear inside your soul any sound of unlawful desire, any noise of restless passion, any dangerous movement of evil impulses and inappropriate inclinations. Don't let any silly or pointless conversation break out in your heart, whether vain fancies, crazy dreams, or images of things as they aren't and shouldn't be. Let the sound of your heart be silence, as if you had forgotten everything whatsoever; as if you were in a place right out of this world, where in quietness and in silence you speak

49

only to me and listen only to my words in your otherwise peaceful heart.

Don't argue with other people, or fiercely maintain your own viewpoint. Let everyone else have their say. If you think someone is wrongheaded, and you can't dissuade him or her by gentle words, or do any good with a mild suggestion or reproach, let him or her go ahead, and decide that you won't argue aloud or by means of your own resentful thoughts, but simply refer the matter to me at once, keeping your heart as quiet as your tongue is peaceful.

4

The contemplative life, which is quite withdrawn from the cares and business of this present world

Keep away from other people as much as you can. Always be alone unless my cause or your neighbour's sake demands your presence, because when you are on your own I shall reveal myself to you. Solitariness, silence, purity and simplicity of heart make a place ready for me to live in. So keep yourself withdrawn from others in silence and quietness of heart. But, when you are alone, don't give in to or even listen to any wrong inclinations, wandering, dreamy thoughts, or pointless desires. I know that you're the sort of person who always looks for consolation; you are always in some way occupied, either outwardly in physical actions, or inwardly by worrying away in your mind, in seeking comfort from the world, with the sole result that you're distracted from what really matters.

So remember to use all your force to withstand your sensual longings and to keep yourself to yourself in outward solitariness of your body and in inward contemplation of your mind – as far as discretion (always a good guide), obedience to your superiors, and charity to your neighbours will allow. Take care, without making a fuss, to avoid all those little ploys which ensure that others keep meeting you. Otherwise you will find it difficult to progress in the spiritual life, which is impeded if you are at the mercy of all and sundry, or all and sundry are at your mercy, and if you're always finding something that you just have to do. But, wherever you are, whether you're with other people or quite on your own, stay with me alone, recollected inside your own soul and withdrawn not only from people and things but even from your own self. By your own self, I mean all impulses to get your own way and pleasure, all concern to get what you want, and all desire to see that your needs and inclinations are satisfied.

Tell yourself that you have been left quite alone in this world and that you have nothing to care for but me, and that you have nothing to think of and no one to deal with but me. Don't start scrutinizing other people's behaviour and don't trouble yourself with their mundane affairs. If you see something which is good – all right – take it in, learn from it. But if you see something evil, leave it alone and say nothing about it; above all don't judge it.

Beware of watching, noting, examining or judging other people's conversation, actions and habits which have nothing to teach you about holiness of life and good example. Go so far as to desire never to hear or understand what such people say. Try not to know them at all. If by accident, or in some situation you can't get out of, you happen to hear what's obviously wrong or useless, root out of your heart the thing heard and the people who say it and try to forget them as soon as possible, especially if there is a danger of offending against charity and of your having and keeping a worse opinion of them than you had before.

5
We ought to judge no one

Don't think the worse of anyone. Even if someone seems really wicked, persuade yourself that he or she has been allowed to fall into what seems evil for some secret and absolutely mysterious reason of my own, so that the person in question will be more humble and become a more wholesome creature in the end. Don't judge, don't despise the apparent evildoer, but instead regret your own ingratitude towards me because my grace and nothing else – against your own will – keeps you from falling. Fill your mind with the thought that without my help you would do things much worse and more reverberatingly awful than anyone else. So tell yourself: If this man or woman had received as much grace as me, he or she would have served God a great deal more devoutly and have been more thankful to him that I have been.

Be quite sure, too, that as soon as I look at that person with the eyes of my mercy, eventually he or she will repent and lead a better life; or else, that he or she already, this very moment, is utterly changed and much holier in fact than those who despise him or her. Ascribe your bad opinion to your own inadequacy and rash judgment, and tick yourself off smartly for having thought the less of your neighbour and done him or her wrong. Rancour, hatred, bitterness and envy often assume the pleasant colours of zeal, and not only make people satisfied to think that their neighbour's every defect and unimportant error are grievously sinful, but persuade them that others' virtues are vices. Remember, even when you keep your sights high they may be dimmed with the foggy mist of malice and envy.

Therefore be especially careful not to check and accuse anyone, and do not speak or listen to talk of anyone's faults when you are angry. Beware, when you are actually in a nasty mood, of trying to gall, wound, oppose, or sadden someone with a neatly chosen word or gesture or facial expression. Don't rebuke people in order to make them feel low and shamefaced. Above all, don't righteously try to take people down a peg or two when you're actually motivated by annoyance, bitterness or some odd and disturbing feeling they arouse in you. Be particularly wary of checking people when your main desire is to make others aware of faults and offences. If that is the case, you can be assured that you have no zeal, love or sincere intention in what you do. If you did, you would be sorry that others had done wrong and try with all your might to excuse and hide from other people your brother's or sister's offence. If he or she had really done something appallingly wrong, you would rebuke them in private, with sorrow in your own soul, and you would pray hard to me for them,

55

suffering with them in your own heart for what they had done. Above all you would feel lovingly towards them and be humbly concerned about them.

Look out for what is wanting in you; try to find the right way for a spouse of mine to behave. Be deaf to others' faults, be dumb as soon as you're tempted to speak about them, and be blind when you see them. If you were in a king's presence all the time and knew his eyes were on you, you would be on your guard, like any bashful virgin. Remember, I am always with you wherever you are, and I am always watching over you. So always be as truly innocent as I have just asked you to be, realizing that I know the very depths of all your actions, thoughts, longings, words, impulses and intentions, and the innermost secrets of your heart.

One thing you always desire is peace of mind. I notice, however, a tendency to let it rely on people's mouths; that is, you tend to be at rest and cheerful when no one opposes you or says anything against you. Instead, peace of mind should depend on me and on a good conscience. Check your desire to be liked, loved and praised by others, and the pleasure you take in that kind of reaction. Let people think and do as people will; just worry about loving me, and whether you are worthy of my approval. Live uprightly with your neighbours and love them for my sake. Be especially wary of the pleasure you get when men who have disapproved of you seem to come round to you again. Leave it all to me.

6

Fighting imperfection

Be tough-minded and on your guard against imperfections, however slight they seem. The least sin that offends me is something that should never seem small to you, if you love me perfectly.

You know best how weak and negligent you are in general, and how reluctant you are to fight your faults and wrongheadedness, to beware of the things that lead you astray, to avoid provocations, to renounce what *you* want, and to do better. You used to be quite determined to change. Get back to that state of mind, and decide to get rid of all your imperfections and to purge yourself of everything that is contrary to my will, of everything that is only a gain in this world.

*   *   *

Whenever you find yourself moved to anger, desire, lust, pride and that kind of thing, stop them breaking out of you in a sudden word or movement. Resist them, suppress them, extinguish them. The best of all remedies against sinful impulses is humbly to throw yourself on my mercy; to remind yourself that you were made from nothing; and that you would be nothing if it weren't for my grace. Turn right round to me. Put all your trust in me. Call on me in prayer. Rest assured that I will help you and that in this kind of distress the only real help you are going to get is from me.

Keep at it. Be afraid that if you decide to give up or if you are just too lazy a person to keep praying, that I won't be able to help you and that I shall, as it were, leave you to your own devices and allow you to take refuge in the most deceitful security – the feeling that anyway you're doing what *you* really want to do. If you feel no self-doubt and you don't move an inch towards me, it is very difficult for me to help you.

People who feel no fear of their own desires are in a very dangerous state. When they think, 'Actually, now I'm doing what I really wanted to do, I feel more relaxed and peaceful than I've ever done', then they're on the edge of the slippery slope. Fight hard against that kind of confidence in your own desires. And never despair.

*   *   *

One thing I have to warn you of especially is your constant tendency to grow faint-hearted under the weight of your faults and oversights, and an inclination almost to despair when a sudden lack of confidence reduces your firm decisions to nothing. I know those moods when you sit there utterly alone, pining, eaten up with unhappiness, in a pure state of grief. You don't move towards me but desperately imagine that everything you have ever done has been utterly lost and forgotten. This near-despair and self-pity are actually a form of pride. What you think was a state of absolute security from which you've fallen was really trusting too much in your own strength and ability. Profound depression and perplexity of mind often follow a loss of hope, when what really ails you is that things simply haven't happened as you expected and wanted.

In fact I don't want you to rely on your own strength and abilities and plans, but to distrust them and to distrust yourself, and to trust me and no one and nothing else. As long as you rely entirely on yourself you are bound to come to grief. You still have a most important lesson to learn: your own strength will no more help you to stand upright than propping yourself on a broken reed. You must not despair of me. You may hope and trust in me absolutely. My mercy is infinite.

What I have said doesn't mean, however, that you should despair in another way; that is, by rejecting your own wits, industriousness, hard work and so on. Use them but don't rely on them.

* * *

What I want from you is daily effort, real humility (no faking here), and continual loyalty to me in struggling against what you know to be wrong. Moreover, I want firm hope, assured trust in my mercy and the kind of constancy that can't be broken down and never decides to stop for a while because of tiredness.

When you find that all these things are there in you, be sure to work for profound humility, the kind that enables you to know yourself perfectly and to acknowledge that, since you were made of nothing by my mercy, you are nothing by my grace, and you have deserved nothing, for your thirst for justice and all the other good things you have, feel and do, come from me.

*   *   *

Complain about yourself to me. As soon as you repent I shall have forgiven you. As soon as you ask me to forgive you I shall have wiped it out and forgotten it all.

So why do you wait to come to me? You can't find safety by running away from me but only by coming straight to me. Wherever you see you have offended most, wherever you find that you have fallen most often, wherever you see that you have gone the greatest distance from virtue, cry most often to me, sigh to me most plaintively, and desire most fervently my forgiveness and my protection.

Resist temptations as much as possible. As long as you resist, you are never a prisoner. Whatever you feel and are forced to suffer – as long as you suffer it against your will, resisting it as I have told you – I shall never find fault with you for that reason. I don't want you to tell me what you feel but what you agree to. It's only natural to feel an impulse to sin in your body, but you are free to consent to it or not. However fiercely the body and the senses are assailed, no one can ever force your will to accept fully what you don't want to accept.

There are two aspects of temptation: one is the thing to which you are tempted; that is, sin and imperfections, to which you must never consent or yield. The other is your hard work and distress in resisting them, which you have to suffer patiently as long as you are tempted.

Of course some people are so weak and unstable that in the very moment when they are getting ready to resist temptation, they fall as it were despite themselves. Completely forgetting what they had decided to do, they begin to contemplate doing what they even refused to think of beforehand. Who can be safe among dangers like these? The only thing that can escape sin unscathed is a good and humble will. What harms chastity for instance is not any impulse or feeling in your body but your actual consent. Whatever is sin must be voluntary, and as long as it is not voluntary, it isn't sin.

Don't be dismayed if even the most loathsome temptations creep into your mind. If they creep in they can creep out again. They can leave by the same way they came in, taking with them anything that is useless and unclean within you, so that they leave your house swept and cleaned.

If you really want to know yourself, and call on me confidently and humbly without any attempt to spare yourself, you will send your enemies packing. As soon as you feel an evil inclination in your mind, remember that you are nothing and that only my grace can help you. Seek aid and protection from my own readiness to suffer for your sake – which now as in the past is what sends the devil packing.

If anyone is overcome, bound and even beaten, and so tightly confined that he can't even move his own limbs, as long as he doesn't admit that he is a prisoner but continues to resist with whatever force he can summon and exert, and never consents to his captivity or his captors, he can never be said to be conquered or overcome. Similarly, I shall never count you as beaten, whether you are tempted by the flesh or the devil, unless you consent with your mind, and cease to resist them. You will find that you feel and have to meet with many things in life that you ought not to admit or consent to, that is, accept with your own will or delight in.

Remember, I am a most upright and just judge. I notice the suffering and labour of every one of my soldiers. I think much more of their will than of their abilities. To be able to conquer is something that you get by my grace alone, but to be willing to conquer is a matter of your own personal choice – even though that, too, cannot be done without my grace.

7

Occasions of temptation

You have to be especially careful to ensure that you yourself are not an occasion of your own temptation or destruction, by giving your enemy, through your own fault, an opportunity to attack you and a means of overthrowing you.

If an enemy who was after your life stood at the door, would you let him in? No, of course not, you would immediately bolt the door, see to all the locks and make sure that all the windows were fastened. Are you, then, going to let all those vicious thoughts into your heart so that they can destroy your inner life? Don't drive me away, but make sure that you keep them out of your house by force, and show how very much you detest them. Turn your heart to me, and if you feel any temptation of body or mind, move your heart away from it.

Punish your body when it seems proud or wayward. Use abstinence and temperance as your weapons, both in food and in drink. Cut off all means of access to persons, all haunting of places, and all using of occasions which you know well tempt you in one way or another. Beware above all else that the devil doesn't use your own body and mind to wound you, as it were, with your own weapons.

Drive out any unclean thoughts which still hammer at you, as it were with one nail after another, by meditating and imprinting on your mind some thought about my life and passion. To think of my life will certainly help you. If I have made sure that all sorts of herbs, stones and roots can yield substances which heal diseases of the body, then I must have given my own sufferings the ability to expel spiritual diseases and to cure and sanctify the soul.

8

Spiritual temptations and when to conquer them

No one with a pure mind needs to be afraid of or to confess evil or unclean thoughts which are borne with grief, not delight, and which one has not yielded to. A holy person will always feel rather soiled by evil ideas that cross the mind, but there is no harm done unless by one's own fault and negligence in yielding to them.

*　　*　　*

The holier the day, and the more earnestly you lift up your heart and strive vehemently to unite yourself wholly to me, the more violently, wickedly and suddenly you will be assaulted by evil ideas, which come either from outside or from some fear of your own. As soon as your soul begins to abhor and fear something, the sooner it will feel and find whatever it is that it fears. Fear and faint-heartedness are the speediest aids to the arrival in the mind of the ideas and images that are most feared.

Evil does its best to entangle your mind with scruples and worries and thus to hinder your peace of mind. Don't take any notice of them, don't fear them, don't resist them, but just continue meditating and praying as though you felt nothing unusual at all and as though your mind were quite untroubled, and pass over all those evil and pointless thoughts as if you had heard a dog barking in the street outside, or a goose hissing, both things no one worries his or her mind about in the least – and certainly doesn't bother to argue with, but just passes by or ignores or at most laughs off. If you do that you will easily avoid and quickly forget them. But if you actively try to resist them, to dispute with them, to take real notice of them, to fear them, to try to get rid of them, you will find that you imprint them all the more deeply in your mind and entangle yourself in worries and depression. These temptations aren't vanquished by fighting with them but by despising them.

You must also be careful that no temptation gets at you by sheer persistence, and by making you too tired to withstand it. This is a customary practice of the devil when he sees that he can affect someone by vexation, by a long and troublesome temptation, who would prove resistant to the most subtle deceits and enticing pleasures. So you have to be long-suffering, constant and patient.

I must also warn you that if you are tempted with physical sins such as gluttony and lust, you can more easily conquer them by running away than by staying to fight. Spiritual vices, on the other hand, are always overcome not by lightly passing over them but by staying with them and thinking a lot about them and

66

doing the exact opposite of what they seek to persuade you to do. Pride, for instance, you get rid of by forcing yourself to do things that will make you humble.

You can overcome envy, in the same way, if you ignore it and do whatever it is that envy tries to dissuade you from; for example, if you are speaking to someone, trying to help, or to behave with humility towards him or her. You can never conquer slothfulness by running away from all work, or by neglecting to serve me and by trying to get out of taking pains with something. You have to use all your might and to apply your whole mind to prayer and devotion in order to overcome laziness.

9
Taking notice of envy

Beware of envy as much as you can. Don't allow it to make you dislike anyone, to speak slightingly of anyone, to put yourself before anyone, to annoy and worry anyone, or to be vexed yourself if anyone is preferred or advanced to your disfavour. Don't be hurt at another person's honour, commendation or spiritual profit.

To overcome this temptation you have to be more courteous and humble towards those whom you are tempted to despise and envy than to others. Say nothing about them and don't listen to anything anyone else says about them in their absence. Never let yourself show the least sign or utter the least sound of envy or anything that springs from the same venomous root.

10

The dangers of eccentricity

When you're talking to others, be careful not to look sad or worried, or to trouble them with words carefully slanted to make them uneasy.

Be careful not to appear eccentric or unusual or 'special'; don't practise your own set of mannerisms or use unnecessary forms of devotion when you are with others. But, as far as things which truly profit your soul are concerned, which your vocation and Christian faith demand, and which are necessary to obtain virtue or avoid sin, don't worry about being the only one to act like that. Don't model yourself on others and on fashion if other people don't care about salvation, but decide for your own soul's benefit humbly to bear all their derision and persecution.

11

Honouring the Mother of God

Pray to my Mother and honour her by trying to imitate her life and virtue. I gave her to this world as a perfect example of holiness, innocence and purity, as a unique and trustworthy refuge for all my servants, and as a sanctuary for all those who are in misery or suffering. I made her so humble, virtuous, merciful, gentle and kind that she would never despise anyone but always show pity to everyone and never allow anyone to leave her without consolation.

Obviously I couldn't have chosen anyone more suitable for this task. The sorrowful, desolate and overwhelmed with their sins, will find this humble and loving woman ready to mediate with me because she is my mother.

12

Feeling religious

It can happen that you just don't feel any real devotion. Don't worry, carry on with a stout and constant mind, even though you feel dry and barren. Do whatever you know honours my cause and do just as much as you can on my behalf. There are a lot of people, after all, who even shed tears and give many signs of always tasting the sweetness of true devotion in their soul, and whose life is not a whit the holier for all that, and can even be in mortal sin. Such people have a certain natural tenderness of heart – I speak not only of women but of men who are by nature passionate and full of compassion, and easily 'feel' devout. The only devotion that counts is devotion which improves your life.

You know the kind of people who start crying immediately they hear that some famous person is dead, even though they've never met him and know nothing about him personally beyond what they've read about him, and even though he may be of some quite alien religion, belief or nation. They will also weep sometimes if they hear about two famous lovers breaking up or one of them dying a tragic death. If people will do that, it's no wonder that they are brought to religious tears at some moving ceremony or just through compassion at my sufferings, or natural rejoicing at some honour they see done to me. Yet all these tears arise from a natural movement of the heart; such people have no virtuous intention in what they do and there is no real profit to their souls, as long as they do not do my will and keep my commandments. So, if you find that your heart is hardened and dried up and you don't feel any emotion, try to have another kind of devotion, by which I mean a true, perfect and ready will, and a determined resolution to do everything that might honour and please me.

In addition, if you're lacking a physical sensation of devotion, it is a good idea to try to find out the real reason. You could have lost that pleasing feeling in your soul because of some silly affection for something or other, or because you've been too occupied with worldly thoughts, or through pride, or by pleasing yourself in this way or that. If that is the case, try being sorry not because you feel empty but for the reason you feel empty: that is, on account of the fault you've committed.

Even if sometimes some little bit of your mind goes on boiling away, or you can't get rid of an annoying scruple of some kind, or something you can't quite define interferes with your devotion, and, of course, if you're distressed, or oppressed by a heaviness of soul, make sure at least that the inward, rational part of you stays peaceful in the assurance that you love my commandments and will try to carry them out.

13
Receiving Holy Communion

When you are going to receive the sacrament of my body and blood, you will sometimes find that you feel no kind of quasi-physical joy or devotion. Don't be discouraged – even if you are suddenly troubled with the most horrible temptations and odious pictures in your mind. It is not necessary for you to *feel* devotion in your soul. What I want is a devotion of your will which enables you to believe that my sacrament is good for you and that even the most blasphemous thought can't separate you from me, and which allows you to honour me even when you *feel* that the sacrament is opposed to your own inclinations and commonsense.

However sad and desolate you feel, even if you are quite downcast when you're going to confession or are walking up the aisle to receive my body, determine to carry on in what you know is good, so that you grow stronger in grace, more constant in goodness, and more fervent in love towards me. A pure intention and a good will will see you through.

Don't be afraid, don't be faint-hearted. Receive me with a quiet mind and a pure conscience, wholly dedicated to my service, desiring to seek me and receive me in the sacrament through which I am and will always remain blessed to you, a most gracious lover, a most gentle protector, a most merciful redeemer, a most loving preserver and a most faithful saviour. That is what you revere, love and desire under the form of bread.

It is the same body that I have glorified in heaven. My body is not dead or bloodless, but holds my soul, my blood, my graces and my virtues. I am one person, yet inseparably united with the other persons of the Trinity in that one person, and so the whole Trinity is present in this sacrament as truly as in heaven, though under a sacramental form. When you receive me in holy communion you receive me really and perfectly; you receive the source of all your happiness.

Don't be afraid, or shy, or too conscientious, or too reverent to receive me. I have asked you to come to receive me in the sacrament to prevent all that. I assure you that I want to be with human beings, and that I rejoice when I do any of you good and can knock at the door of your hearts, come in and eat with you, and feed and refresh your hungry spirits with myself. The only reason why I do all this is to ensure that you hope and trust in me.

14

Discretion

Humility should guide you in all your prayer and devotion. They should also be ruled and moderated by discretion, so that they don't harm you in any way or make you unable to do your duty. There is no point in allowing outward exercises which are so good or profitable to hinder the inward actions of your spirit, and no virtuous act should ever offend against basic charity.

*   *   *

You must also take care of your health. If you're feeling weak, don't consume your strength. Your plans, devotions and exercises should be governed by that thought. Take advice from your superiors or from obviously good people in this respect, and stop or reduce, increase or moderate your devotion as they advise you. If your spiritual director or superior – who is my deputy, as it were, in charge of your soul – forbids you to fast or recommends anything which isn't sinful, obey him or her.

If you are told to eat eight times a day, for example, you won't offend me by doing so. All you have to do is to retain a will to fast when you have recovered and are able to make your own choice in the matter. If you eat for obedience' sake, you will receive a double reward from me. Your good will to fast and the fruit of your good will are not lost if you eat to show your obedience to what is for your own good. It is the same with all things which you would like to do, and are usually good for you, but which you have to give up under obedience.

Try every day to advance my glory as much as possible wherever you can, and to do my will in yourself and in others. Don't neglect any good work that you have the ability to do, but try to do better every day without glorying or rejoicing in your own ability or all the effort you put into being good. Remember that you should act as if you did nothing entirely of yourself.

Some people are not content with the hardship that I offer them but torment their bodies with indiscreet abstinence and immoderate suffering. In that way they make themselves unable to obey me, to follow my example, and to withstand the conflicts of the spiritual battle. Their natural strength is used up so that they can't effectively carry out the actions and devotions they were used to before, and take more care of their bodies than they need to or is convenient for them, going well beyond what is necessary to repair the ravages caused by their own folly. So moderate your exercises and labours in accordance with your strength and ability, taking care not to overstrain and thereby defeat yourself. Don't neglect to nourish your body with some food and drink. It is my will that you should comfort nature and from time to time build yourself up – not with fancy things or out of delight in the extraordinary, but just in order to refresh your natural state.

I also want you to enable your body to serve me more aptly, to make yourself a fit instrument of my grace, to fulfil my will, to follow my commandments and to do those works which I find acceptable. I want you always to be ready, if it pleases me, to suffer poverty as much as to enjoy riches, and to be as willing to be sick as to be healthy. But when discretion doesn't compel you to nourish your body out of natural weakness, be careful lest by impatience or lack of devotion, or out of an insatiable desire to please your own appetite, you look for all kinds of excuses to escape from the adversities and troubles which I send you. Remember to accept gladly the crosses I send you. Suffer them patiently, don't complain about them to anybody, bear them with long-suffering and humbly persist, being assured that I shall be pleased with you and what you do.

15

Following Jesus Christ in everything

A faithful spouse ought to be so loving towards her husband that she desires with all her heart to be with him always, never without him and at no time absent from him. She should want to go along with him in all things good and to be glad about being like him for he is a good person to be like. You should behave in the same way towards me. Think about my life, actions and virtues so that you can discover what I love and what I find pleasing in you.

Loving soul, if you want to be a faithful spouse of Jesus Christ, you ought to desire nothing so much as to please me and to model yourself in all things in accordance with my will and to do whatever I find right and good. Wherever I go, therefore, go with me. Whatever I do, do your best to imitate me. Whatever I suffer, be ready to suffer with me. And if in any circumstances you are worried or feel hard done by, rejoice in it, because it makes you like me.

16

Poverty

Remember my poverty first. When I was rich I made myself poor for your sake. Think how I came to my own people and they did not receive me. I was very poor and like a stranger and a traveller in a foreign land. My mother had to put up in an inn, as a guest in a strange place. I was born in a stable near the mouths of animals, the heat of whose breath was my defence against the bitter cold. I was laid upon hay in a manger. I was saved by the sacrifice of poor innocents. When I was an infant I was driven into banishment. I was brought up by my mother's labour and fed by alms spared by others from their own hard-won earnings, and had no house or lodging of my own. I often went out to meditate alone in the mountains. My clothes were taken from me during my passion and I died naked on the cross, being in so great want of all things that even in my most extreme thirst I could not get a drop of water to wet my parched tongue. Lastly, after my death, I was buried in a grave dug for another.

How often do you consider how in the whole course of my life I suffered hunger, cold, thirst and other vexations of my body? As for physical consolations – which most people think very necessary – I utterly rejected them, patiently enduring penury and poverty in all things. But you, when you have everything that you can desire to hand, nevertheless flatter yourself and imagine that you are living in poverty, and make the most enormous fuss if you can't have everything that you want, even when it is really superfluous and needed more to please your envious mind than to serve your actual needs.

So look at my poverty and stop being depressed, and cease being offended if you see anyone given some advantage over you or with more than you have. Why aren't you sad instead to see anyone poorer than yourself, like St Francis? If you happen to meet anyone (and you ought really to think like this of everyone) who follows my life and poverty more closely than you do, it should not make you unhappy because others are happy or better than you, but heartily sorry because you aren't good yourself, and that the reason is your own fault and negligence.

So rejoice and take it as a special sign of my grace and a great benefit, if I make you more agreeable to me than others, by sending you some terrible sickness, some extreme poverty, misery, misfortune, or contempt in this world. If you want things that are necessary, rejoice. Be glad if they are taken away and don't complain about it to anyone, but together with me embrace the cross of poverty, being quiet and contented in your mind, remaining silent and utterly renouncing your own self.

Decide now, and make a firm resolution from the bottom of your own heart, to despise all things for the love of me, and be unwilling to possess anything but whatever necessity forces you to have and to use, delighting in all poverty, contempt, and penury, so that you may be utterly worthy to enjoy me. Since I am better for you than a thousand worlds, I ought to be more esteemed and more dearly beloved by you than all earthly things whatsoever. Why do you dally, my daughter? Be encouraged by my example. Be inflamed with my love. In everything that has to do with your self, try earnestly to live in want and poverty. And whatever you have, treat as belonging to others, so that you neither love it when you possess it, nor are grieved by it when you lose it. Whatever you do enjoy, treat as given to you for other people's use and to serve their needs.

17

Humility

Detest and abhor with all your heart the honour, glory and favour of human beings, together with all other flatteries and enticements of this deceitful world. Do not think in any other way of yourself than as a proud person who is ungrateful to me, spiteful against me, and therefore, if I were to reward you as you deserved, worthy to be hated by all creatures as one unworthy to be carried by the earth, to receive breath from the air, or to be fed and served by any of my creatures. Therefore, always ask me for mercy and grace, not relying on any work or merit of your own, but trusting wholly in the one work of redemption which I carried out for you, and that insurpassable mercy which I showed towards you. Desire with tears and sorrow my gift of perfect humility, so that it will enable you to delight in remaining hidden and unknown, despised and thought nothing of.

Don't glory in anything and don't boast about or be proud of anything that you have, feel or do. If anyone happens to offend or to despise you, don't be angry with that person, or look sourly at him or her, or bear him or her less or no good will. Instead be quite astonished that every creature alive doesn't persecute you in return for the injury that you have done to me who made both you and them, and whom you nevertheless aren't in the least afraid to offend.

18

Obtaining humility

In order to obtain humility, consider my majesty, omnipotence, wisdom and goodness: I who alone am immortal and infinite beyond all measure, without any limitation or circumscription, beyond the power of human words to describe, incomprehensible, the one from whom all creatures receive their existence, and who am able – just like that – to bring all creatures and the whole world to nothingness, and then immediately to restore everything to its former course and order. Therefore, since you see that I have such great power in every respect, you may easily see too that I created you rational creatures in my own image and likeness, not out of necessity or for any need which I had of you, but out of my love and goodness towards you, as persons to whom I wanted to give my good things and my happiness.

It was from that grace that you fell by sin, making yourselves unworthy of eternal life and putting yourselves into a state of eternal suffering. I who became a human being for your sakes suffered thirty-three years of hunger, thirst, cold, heat, miseries, labours, persecutions, contempt, scars, blows, wounds, griefs, torments and lastly the cross and death itself, so that I might deliver you from eternal deadness which you had decided to accept. My daughter, I lived in the world not as a God, not as a mighty person or in glorious state, but as the poorest, least important, most despised and unworthy of human beings, subject to many sufferings and reproaches, until in the end I was murdered in the most shameful and ignominious way – a death which the world thought I richly deserved. People judged my life and teachings to be so detestable that they tried their best to root them out of all human memory and to make them come to an end with my death, at which a great crowd of people triumphed and rejoiced.

Yet I suffered all that as gladly as a thirsty animal drinks when it has found water. Indeed, I was so drunk with my love for you, that I ran towards my death and never felt truly myself and healthy until I had suffered it. I did not spare myself, and I did not run away from any labour, grief, pain or torment whatsoever. I refused to do nothing which might help you and do you good. You were so dear and precious to me that I was even full of a great longing to give myself up for your sake to be wounded in every way with all kinds of tortures, and for your sake, too, at the last, to end my life with a shameful death. In addition, because I had a terrible thirst for your salvation, I wanted to shed all my blood for you, and did so so plentifully that there wasn't a single drop left in my body.

Can't you see that I am no longer able to withhold my mercy from you? Don't you see how I have called you, and where I have put you? What have you done? What have you achieved? Can't you realize how I forget all your wrongs, idiocies and ungratefulness?

I don't say all this, my daughter, to concentrate proudly, as it were, on the benefits you have had from me and all the good I have heaped on you, but because I languish with love for you, and seem to stand in need of you, even though I am in need of nothing. Since it seems as if I am not able to live without you, I beg you to love me again because of the unlimited goodness and love which I have shown you, so that by loving me you may perfectly see what I am, and what you are, how much I have done for you, and how you have hurt me in return for all that I have done for you.

If you were to think right down inside yourself about the great poverty, low status and contempt which I – infinitely mighty, rich, dignified, immeasurably majestic, infinitely good and incomprehensibly so – was prepared to suffer in order to serve you, who have done things which make you scarcely worth the description human, and if you were to think properly about the great love, faithfulness and longing with which I suffered for you; those harsh thoughts would fill your heart with such obedience, reverence, and desire to serve and adore me, that no one could ever express your intention in words or conceive it in thoughts. Real contemplation of what I have done would fill you with an insatiable desire and burning thirst to honour me, to worship me, to exalt me and to humble and despise yourself and, for the love of me, to throw yourself beneath the feet of all my creatures, and then patiently to suffer reproaches, contempt and hurt at their hands.

However greatly you humble yourself, however much you suffer, you must realize that you have suffered nothing in regard to the thirst and desire you feel in your own mind to humble yourself and to exalt me. You should love most of all those who seek most to oppress and despise you, because this helps you to satisfy your real desire and your humility, for they are wholly intent on humbling and abasing you. If you still don't feel these things in yourself, recognize how unthankful you are, and how far from true humility, which is a sincere, pure and lowly submission of your heart in the sight of my divine majesty. You must also think little of your own self and decide firmly to welcome the contempt of others.

I ask you once again to look at my own humility and to follow that example in your own life. See how the world despised my life and teachings; how people falsely accused and utterly rejected me; how they criticized me in all their speeches; how I suffered great reproaches, scorn, contempt and derision, and even quite degraded people said whatever they wanted about me. Though I was mocked and was made the despised object of anyone's scorn, I despised no one. I did not excuse myself or say anything to resist or reprove my accusers and persecutors. Think of your own obstinacy, negligence, sins, ingratitude, inconstancy, lowliness, and last of all, how you are nothing of yourself but something only by my grace. Bewail, lament and excuse yourself for all these things with continual sorrow. Turn whatever happens to you to your own benefit and use it as a means to make yourself humble. Make sure that you do not take pleasure in yourself but wonder instead how you could ever please or delight anyone else who really knows you as you are. Always fix the eyes of your heart on your own weakness and disability in all respects.

Consider how you are nothing and what you ought to be and are not. Also think of what you do not have and how unable you are to do any good; how many things you lack; and in short how far you are from true and perfect charity, and from the perfection of a holy person's life. Call to mind also how unlike me you are and remember that of yourself you have nothing that is any good at all, but that you receive everything that is good from me alone and by no other means whatsoever. Moreover, you are the sole source of a readiness to sin, to offend, to rebel, to stand in need of everything that is good, to be in necessity and misery, and by your own fault to lose and cast away all those blessings and graces which I give you.

It is quite certain that if I were to leave human

nature to do as it wished, it would do no good at all, but decline daily from bad to worse. Human nature is nothing of itself and works hard to achieve nothing at all. Think about all this; I assure you that it is the best way to gain humility.

19

We shouldn't worry about what others think of us

Don't spend your time worrying about what other people think of you or whether they are running you down. There is no need to trouble yourself about how people sum you up, unless you knowingly offend them or give them reason to rebuke you or gossip about you. You will not be any better off if they praise you, or any worse off if they criticize you. So don't be overjoyed when others commend you, or wounded when they find you lacking. After all, what do you gain from the praise of others? Nothing, in fact. But it does you a great deal of harm, deceiving you and blowing you up with pride and vanity. Furthermore, how can contempt, dressing down, making you feel small, talking behind your back, condemnation and persecution hurt you? In no way. Instead, you should welcome them because they help you to realize what you're really like, and because they can do something to make you think less of yourself and to change your behaviour. At any rate, these things will make you more careful and prudent when you talk to people, and suggest to you that you should trust not them, but me.

Human judgment isn't worth your worries, whether people speak good or evil of you. Let them think whatever they want. In the meantime lift up your heart to me. If you search every corner of your heart and find nothing there to offend me, there is nothing to be afraid of. But if you look into yourself and find something that has offended me, be sorry about it: not because people despise you, for that is something you ought to put up with, but because you have offended me and have given other people an example of wrong behaviour. If anyone happens to praise or criticize something about you which isn't sinful, don't let it affect you more than when you hear someone else praised and criticized.

If people praise you, put it down to their error and mere good will towards you. If they reprove or condemn you, don't be astonished. Is it any wonder if people reprove, despise and condemn your life, seeing that they also reproved my life and condemned all my teachings, which were most innocent, without any spot or stain, and against which no one in their right senses or with the least good will could bring any objection whatsoever? Rejoice instead that you are following the same road that I took before you: the way, that is, of being humbled and treated as nothing by everyone, and be glad that you suffer these trials from others. Let others think up things to annoy and harm you. I shall turn their mischief to your benefit. Just put up with it all patiently, and keep quiet.

Try always to please me and not other people. If you do happen to please people, then believe that they are deceived about your real nature, because they don't know you as well as I do, but judge you straightforwardly and guilelessly by the appearance of goodness which you affect in front of them. But if you happen to displease them, remember that you deserve it, and let it make you more humble. If they despise you for the tiny faults they can see in you, what would they say and do if they saw as perfectly as I do all your sins and offences? Delight in being thought of as contemptible, and however much you are despised think that you deserve to be despised a great deal more than that.

Be careful when you pray to me and ask me for things, that you don't think of yourself but only of me, in case you fall into pride. Remember that you're nothing of yourself, how quickly you fall when I don't protect you, and how you're unable to stand the least temptation when I'm not fighting for you.

You are too ready to run down others, which is a certain sign of your essential arrogance, as though you were worthy to be preferred before those you run down, perhaps because you think you're without the vice you see in them – and forget that you're controlled by many other vices. If you weren't blind, you might be able to see that you don't deserve at all to be favoured instead of those others, but that your own tongue makes you much more detestable than them, because it makes your arrogance and envy plain to anyone in the world with sense to see it. My friends usually accuse themselves of their own vices and don't find fault with others, for they suspect the things they do and themselves; and they can't trust themselves in anything because they have so often been deceived when they've done so. They're always afraid that they're not looking for me as sincerely as they ought to. Besides, they admire and praise other people's actions, and won't be persuaded to think evil of anything that others do. Remember to praise or to excuse others, or else say nothing at all, always keeping before your eyes your own nothingness and ungratefulness, and just be astonished that everyone you meet doesn't reprove and detest you.

20

Obedience

Obedience is a first-class virtue. It is something I find most acceptable. Just think of something which is the very least of actions – if it is done merely for the sake of obedience, it is more worthwhile to the person that does it than an infinite number of other deeds which people do willingly and to please their own appetites and likings. You can't offer me a more perfect sacrifice than a humble heart which is obedient and ready to do everything which I command. Someone may by the exercise of obedience alone forsake himself or herself for my sake, and thus profit more by denying the will than by spending a great amount of time on the most noble exercises.

So always try to be as obedient to me as if I were always bodily present in the room with you, and as if you continually enjoyed my presence in the way of a wife who always has her husband with her. If anyone calls you away from me to do something which counts as an act of obedience, then you ought to leave me and obey that person – because then you please me by preferring my will before your own comfort.

Learn to leave yourself for my sake, that is, by denying your own will. Think that nothing is so precious and nothing so profitable that you can't be taken away from it for obedience' sake with a mind wholly resigned to my pleasure. Whatever the thing is, if you love it so much you refuse obedience, or are grudgingly or unwillingly obedient, that thing is the very idol of your own longings and appetites, and more harmful to you than can be expressed in words. If you are in a place where you have no superior or where you yourself are the superior, make everyone else your superior, obeying their will and forsaking your own.

Love the virtue of obedience from the bottom of your heart and don't neglect it as long as you live, not only in regard to your superiors, but whenever you are not held back by my will, in all things and to all people for my sake, and without being upset, grumbling about it, or arguing about it. So that you can do this the more sincerely, don't respect the person who by my command is set above you, whether he or she is learned or unlearned, an excellent or a base person. Think only of the fact that he or she has been made your superior by my providence, and that through that person you ought to hear me, ask my advice and obey me.

So don't resist but yield to my providence, for if I appoint someone over you, I am concerned for your well being, however learned or simple the person is. So, no scruples. Despise your own wisdom and submit yourself to be advised and judged.

Whatever opinions are offered you should accept as

if they came from me. Do nothing without the spiritual advice of your pastor or confessor or superior. Always live in simplicity and poverty of spirit, renouncing your own judgment, your own advice, your own sharp analysis, and your own opinion. Don't complain or murmur, but treat as the best opinion whatever your superior says or, if you have none, whatever others say, as long as it is not clearly or to all intents and purposes sin.

You should distrust your own will so much that you live among others as if you had no will of your own, as if you chose nothing more than another, but accepted indifferently all things that happened to you, except that someone else's opinion must please you more than your own, if only there is no sin in it and you can find honesty and discretion in it. Yield to others in all things which are yours, in, that is, everything that has to do specially with you, as if you had professed obedience to them all. Whenever you are alone, don't do your own will, but act as far as your own self is concerned as if the whole course of your life and all your exercises were set towards the renunciation of self.

21

Mortifying our own wills and desires

The only thing that can do you real harm is your own will. As soon as you have mortified it, no one else can hurt you. It's obvious that no living thing can harm you if you are dead to yourself and if you have mortified your own desires. If you have deadened these words in yourself: 'I', and 'me', and 'to me', and 'mine', that is, if you have no desire whatsoever to please yourself, who can hurt you, for then I live in you and you in me, and no creature can resist me but all things that are must serve me? If you are determined to follow your own will, then everything will resist you and fight against you, and, whether you want it or not, in the end there is no way in which you can escape my providence – though it will prove a cross to you and not a consolation that brings you great joy.

If you entirely renounce your own will, you will taste an inward peace and joy which your own physical appetite and longings cannot imagine. You will be distressed by the things of this world – but be confident, for I have overcome the world, and therefore you can overcome it through me and thus find peace. So pluck up by the roots all the desires of the world and all self-love from your heart. Otherwise, how can you overcome the world and the devil if they have their army inside you? – that is, if they have their vices living inside your soul? Throw out quickly whatever you have inside you which is contrary to my will, and whatever opposes you in your spiritual battles. Neither the world nor the devil can ever vanquish you or resist you unless they are helped by the things they own inside you.

The less control your own appetite has over you, the more interest I still have in you, and the farther you banish your own desires from you, the more fully I possess you. If you follow your own will it will not allow me to work in you. It deprives you of me who am infinite goodness itself. However hard you work, and whatever clever ploys you think up, you will never find any other way to come to me than what I taught my disciples: 'If anyone wants to follow me, that person must deny himself or herself, forsaking his or her own will and taking up a cross to follow me'. Whatever you give up, if you don't give up your own self, you have given up nothing. Similarly, if you don't possess your own self, but leave yourself to be possessed by me, you have given up everything for my sake, even though you live in great wealth and honour. The more you go out of yourself, the more I enter into you, and the more you die to yourself, the more I live in you.

So forsake everything in order to find everything. Forsake yourself in order to find me. All your worries come only from that extreme self-love which holds your heart, and from your lack of confidence in me. Forsake yourself and believe me. Do you think that I can deceive you? Why don't you commit yourself to me? Why don't you trust in my goodness? What good can you do for yourself of yourself? What are you without me? Are you in danger if you commit yourself to me and renounce your own will? If you commit yourself to me you will never be sick. I can't reject you, I can't forsake you, I can't deceive you and I can't but love you. Throw yourself into my arms and rely wholly on me with confidence and without delay. I shall receive you and look after you. Without me you are as if you did not exist at all. So, if you love yourself, reject yourself and embrace me so that I may also embrace you. Unite yourself closely with me, so that no one can hurt or even touch you without of necessity first hurting and touching me.

Do you want to know how much you have forsaken yourself, or how much you have mortified your own will? When the loss of anything, when reproaches, when injuries happen to you, see if they trouble you and if they trouble you more when they happen to you than when they happen to others. In this way you will judge the love you have for others, and the degree of affection you have for yourself. You love worldly goods, honour, peace, and miserable and transitory things, because you love yourself. You want to enjoy these things, whereas, if you loved me, you would rather banish all those things from your heart for my sake, and suffer all hardship as willingly as you would possess happiness. You should not be more but rather less troubled when adversities happen to you, than when they happen to others. You should never be worried by anything that happens in this world, unless you are irreverent or contemptuous to me.

Anything that you feel in yourself which doesn't come from me, whatever alters or possesses your mind, whatever image of anything at all works hard to imprint itself in your heart, whatever tries to make you like it or to grieve or take you over, is something that you must try with a recollected mind, close shut within itself and lifted up to me, lightly to pass over and carelessly to despise. You should despise all hope and fear, gain and loss, quiet and labour, joy and grief, joy and sadness, and all things that try to take possession of your heart, and all the affection you have for them. If you fix your mind on me, you will easily tread all these things under your feet. But if you love yourself, and if you have not wholly renounced your own self, you will always feel when you follow your own appetite, joy and grief, anger and fear, worry and an infinite number of other passions.

You can never be peaceful unless you have completely mortified yourself, and have quite forgotten your own self. You must wholly abandon yourself so that you may live in me wholly, and make yourself wise only in me, and be sensitive to nothing but to me alone. You will want for nothing if you are content to want yourself in this way. You will want for nothing as long as you are with me. I shall look after you, I shall protect you. You can lose nothing if you lose yourself in this way, for in me you will find something a hundred times better than what you have lost for my sake.

22

God's providence

As long as there is any choice or inclination in you which persuades or tempts you to take more pleasure, to be better contented and to receive greater consolation from one thing than from another, you still have something of your own in you, and you have not yet fully renounced your own self. You ought to treat all things indifferently and equally, without more joy or grief at one time than at another, and to rely and depend only on my providence. This course will give you the greatest liberty, peace and rest for your soul.

So don't rely on yourself. Don't believe your own clever mind or rely on your own strength. Don't trust in your own ability. Promise yourself nothing of your own power, don't build on your own imagination and do nothing that you have invented out of your own head. Don't trust in your own will, even when what you will is good. Forsake yourself in everything, go out of yourself, and renounce all the possessions you have in your own self, so that you rest and repose in me entirely, trust in my goodness, and rely on my grace and on my providence. Be ready always without any choice, any difference and any murmuring or complaining in your heart, to receive adversity as willingly as prosperity, for my sake, desiring always to do no more or less than my will.

Don't trouble your heart with any thoughts about the future. Don't worry about things that are uncertain and may happen, but leave all these things to me who governs everything. It may happen that the evil which is feared or expected may not occur, or if it does happen, well, sufficient for the day is the evil thereof. Whatever happens to you by my permission, my providence ought to please you above everything else, and you ought to praise me for it, and to hold it as an undoubted truth that whatever happens to you like that is what is best for you, and that it was foreseen and arranged by my hand, to happen to you for your own good. Thinking well of me and trusting firmly in me are, as it were, trumpets on which people sound my goodness. Therefore, when I find these things in people, they please me so much that I can never forsake them or allow anything evil or dangerous to happen to them if they have firmly decided to hope in me.

The greater hope and trust that you have in me, the more fully and perfectly you will obtain what you really desire. Whatever happens to you, if you believe that I am so good that I will turn all your problems and hardships and everything that oppresses you and all your persecutors and enemies to your good, that is, to your benefit, I shall not deceive you, but in fact do so. If you can put yourself in the state of mind that accepts things like that, then that is certainly what will happen.

If by my grace you overcome the excessive love for yourself which you have inside you, and confidently commit yourself to me, you will find that my grace works wonders in you. Think of me. Clean forget yourself. Then I shall think continually of you and never forsake you.

Try to find in everything you see and feel and in all things that happen to you, some reason to praise and honour me, so that you may be worthy to understand the true reason why I permitted them, that is, with what great love I sent them to you, and how you ought to refer all these things to my pleasure, to trust in me and to offer yourself for my glory, to the fountain from which they flowed – to my goodness. If you knew how to find me in every single thing and individual that I have made, there would be nothing that could seem contrary to you or contrary to my nature, and everything would make you ready to offer yourself to me, for I am in every creature, and without me no creature can have any being.

23

We have to suffer troubles and hardship

Accept troubles and tribulations as signs of my grace. Whenever you are oppressed with any worry or difficulty, rejoice, knowing that you have deserved it. Don't ascribe what you are suffering to anyone or anything but your own sins. Thank me for being so merciful as to visit and reprove you like my very own child, and not utterly reject you. As long as I trouble you, that is a sign that I want you to do better. But If I withdraw my correction, leaving you wholly to yourself and to shift for yourself, then you will think that you are at peace and resting and unworried, but in reality you will be absolutely unhappy, for then I have taken away from you the care and regard which I had for you.

Whatever trials you suffer, say to yourself: I have deserved a much worse punishment. Even if you have deserved none, bear with all the trials I send you, for the love of me and for my own sake, for I suffered much for your sake.

Remember that you are mine, created and made by me, and no less in my power to be shaped in every way according to my will than clay in the potter's hand. It is in my power and part of my justice to do with you whatever I wish, and it is no more permissible for you to gainsay me than for the clay to resist the potter. What have you to say against me, your Creator, whether I send you comfort or sorrow? But since you have done so many regrettable things, you should want your arrogance to be humbled.

There is another reason to move you: I love you most loyally and provide things which are best and wholesome for you. Since it was my will before I created you that you should suffer at this moment the same things which you are suffering, you ought to desire my loving will to be fulfilled in you, and endure all those things which you suffer with gladness, with a sweet kind of patience, with thanksgiving, with meekness and with devotion in your heart, with no harsh or bitter thoughts against those who try to make you suffer in these various ways. Instead you should treat them as my messengers, fix your eyes on me, and think how loving, kind and faithful is my heart in sending you these troubles for your benefit.

Remember that no one reaches eternal glory except by the cross and cup of affliction and that there is no other way but this highway to the heavenly country. You just have to take that way if you want to enjoy my company in eternal happiness. There is nothing so small or worthless which you do or suffer for my sake that will not receive a very great and glorious reward from me. Yet, I don't want you to serve me or to suffer all these things just because you are going to be rewarded, but only out of sheer love towards me. I know what reward I shall give you. All my gifts are of free grace.

Don't be so base-minded as to linger on the thought of reward but think of me with a more noble, loving and faithful heart and submit yourself to me, out of love for my own sake, and suffer whatever I decide to lay on you. If you knew what great fruit came from tribulations, you would find it a great happiness to glory in crosses and troubles. The greater the adversities that happen to you, and the more they are contrary to your desires, even if they seem to contradict your desire to please me, try the more earnestly and patiently to suffer them. It is my will that your will should sometimes be hindered, even when it is good, so that for one virtue you may receive two, and for the troubles which hindered your will you may obtain a crown of patience.

Don't blame other people if troubles come along. People are my instruments – why blame them? Don't argue with or against them, be worried instead that your own impatience might harm you. Be courteous and gentle to all people and take patiently whatever happens. Keep your features mild and behave humbly, so that no anger, annoyance, complaints, dejected thoughts or sorrow appear in, on or about you, and there is nothing in or apparent in you which might make people think that you were suffering some affliction or were oppressed by some care or difficulty.

If anyone reproaches or criticizes you, look mild and behave gently, keep your peace, and smile bashfully and modestly to show your charity which accepts everything in good part and takes all things well, without either thinking of revenge or remembering harm done. Be careful at such times not to speak more than two or three words, and do so very temperately. Be so humble that no one is afraid to reprove, displease or reproach you. When anyone checks or criticizes you, learn to keep silent, to bear it patiently, and then you will certainly find my grace, which you can never have by any other means than by being quiet, and suffering patiently whatever I send to try you, so that you are as willing (if I please) to receive troubles as to enjoy prosperity.

Follow my example, and don't murmur or complain. Don't fight for yourself, or answer back. Don't defend or excuse yourself. Hold your peace and commit yourself and your cause to my protection. I shall fight for you.

Keep close to me in all quietness without any perturbation or commotion in your soul, being ready quite gladly to suffer any confusion for my sake rather than inwardly in your mind or outwardly in your appearance to murmur in the least way against me. As long as you believe that you have been wronged, as long as you think that you have suffered unjustly, or that you have not deserved the things you are suffering, you have not reached true patience, or a perfect knowledge of yourself.

I want you always to be ready with a joyful and devout heart to run and meet any pain or adversity which happens to you, and to offer yourself to me as willing to suffer hardship and bear misery. Think any day wasted on which you have not received some cross. I was an innocent lamb without any bitterness to those who spat on me, scourged me and crucified me. I excused them and prayed for them. Do likewise. Believe that nothing injurious could happen to you.

There is nothing which cannot be a means for you to obtain my grace more abundantly. You will find me in every one of them. Contemplate people and things not as the creatures they are but me in those creatures. Then you will receive me, hear me, feel me in every one of my creatures, for I speak to you in all of them. Learn by everything that happens to you what I want you to do, and when you know my will be ready to do it. If you do that, then the world and everything that is in it should be a book of instruction to help you do what pleases me most.

24

When consolation is lacking

The best road that has been taken by all my best friends, and the one that you must follow too, is to lack all kinds of consolation, to be surrounded with adversity and disress on every side, and to be so poor that there is nothing left to which you can turn for help and comfort, go to for refuge, or in which you can trust; no one you ask for advice, or trust in, but me. Then you must reflect my glory in suffering those afflictions inwardly in your mind and outwardly in your behaviour, by serving all others and subjecting yourself to them, as if it were permissible for them (without committing any offence or doing you any injury) to afflict you and to tread you under their feet. And there is another perfection: to be destitute of all earthly and heavenly consolation, to be laden with temptations, distress, vexations, doubts, fears, perplexities and adversities, and to be as it were utterly rejected by me and quite forgotten by me, and yet not to leave me for the things I have made, nor even to desire consolation and explanations, but still to trust me, to expect patiently my pleasure, to keep close to me with pure faith and perfect charity, and to be ready to stay like that as long as I permit it, even when you have a dry and barren heart.

25

Inward peace and meekness of heart

You should understand now how you ought to be patient and in patience meek; that is, how you ought to suffer all things with an indifferent, peaceable and quiet mind. Meekness is no more than perfect tranquillity and true patience. Nothing should be able to make you sad or to vex or trouble you, but you must always resolve never to be excluded from my grace and charity and never in your own will be withdrawn or divided from me.

You must also remember, wherever you are, and whatever pain or consolation you feel, to rejoice in it and to do whatever is my will, whether you are comforted or afflicted. If you think that, then no loss of any external thing that could happen to you in this world can ever really make you grieve. Nothing can happen that is contrary to your real desires so long as my will is always your will. It should be the greatest possible joy for you when my will is done in you, then you are fully composed in your most inward self and being, in all peace and tranquillity, even though your outward self is distressed and desolate.

26

Loving our neighbour

Your heart should be filled with compassion and chaste love for your neighbour. Love is chaste when it doesn't stain the heart with lust, isn't too familiar, and doesn't disquiet the heart with thoughts that distract your soul and trouble it with vain desires, or fill your imagination with all sorts of fancies and pictures of a hundred and one things. It is chaste when, without choice of persons or regard to sex, it embraces all kinds of men and women for my sake, with great love and for the sake of love alone, and for no other reason at all.

You should always flow with a general compassion which can never stop running. Be sorry for everyone in their needs and trials, pour out your kindness, affability, mercy and pity on all people. Comfort them and help them to bear their troubles, treating their worries as your own, and acting as a tender mother towards all you meet. Excuse everyone, and do them good by your prayers, and all that is good that you can do for them. If you can't really help anyone directly, try to lessen their sorrow with kind behaviour, loving words and any other means you can think of.

Be very, very careful not to judge or despise anyone, because that harms your soul and displeases me greatly. Never suspect or think ill of others. Excuse all who fall and offend. If you see someone sin, say inside yourself that I allowed him or her to fall so that the conversion could be all the greater, that there was a good intention, and that this person was deceived by ignorance or error; that he or she was weak and too strongly attacked by temptation and therefore forced to yield. Say sincerely in your heart that you would have fallen much more seriously if the same temptation had attacked you. You should never look at your neighbour's actions from just one viewpoint, but examine both your own and your neighbour's actions from different angles. Judge your own deeds with a severe eye, exaggerating your own imperfections, and never puffing up your own virtues.

Reckon your neighbour's imperfections as very small indeed, and his or her virtues as very great. And never speak or hear ill of others. Never reprove a neighbour in anger, even when there is reason for blame. What does it profit you if you cure another and wound yourself? What use is the medicine if you heal one wound and then cause others? Say to yourself that a time will come when you will have an opportunity to reprove your neighbour, and then be lenient and gentle, entreating and exhorting but never handling sharply or roughly. And pray to me to make your reproof effective.

Never be the cause of dissension or the breeding of dissension, discord, or hatred among people, but let everything you say tend to peace. I have said: 'Blessed are the peacemakers, for they shall be called the children of God'. If anyone offends you, or persecutes you with malice, requite these wrongs with benefits, answer hard and sour looks with sweet and meek behaviour, and sharp and reproachful words with mild and gentle remarks, and by this means bring others more easily to realize what wrong they have done.

27

Purity of heart

Try to make your heart so pure that you are withdrawn from all earthly considerations, and are not attached to any pleasure. Try not to delight or find delight in anything, or to be happy with desiring any pleasure whatsoever. Cut off not only unlawful thoughts, but all idle and useless thoughts too, allowing none of them to enter your heart or mind. Think nothing but of me or for my sake.

Look at nothing, whether far distant from prayer, or deformed or contrary to all goodness, without trying to find some reason in it to pray to me and to praise my name. Let everything be a means for you to lift up your heart to me. If you see something beautiful, pleasant or delightful, acknowledge that it comes from me, and let it remind you of my beauty and glory, so that I am your whole delight and consolation. Let all things edify you and whatever happens to you use as an opportunity to meditate on something that is profitable to your soul.

28

All the good things we receive are to be referred to the goodness of God

Never rejoice in yourself or be glad for your own sake at any good thing, or that you have done a good thing. Rejoice in me and in my goodness, liberality, gentleness and mercy to an unworthy and unthankful creature.

Rejoice in my gifts without attributing any praise to yourself, and ascribe the whole glory to me. Behave discreetly in receiving my gifts (except for thankfulness and humility) and as if nothing had been given you, nothing done in you, and you felt no good at all. Look at your own unworthiness and remember that of yourself you are nothing. Remember that of yourself you can do nothing, and your own imperfection, which cannot manage the smallest goodness without my grace. Don't be conceited, or rejoice in your own ability, or flatter yourself with your own power, but attribute everything to me.

If you feel any marvellous inspiration within, or the power of my grace in you, or that by my mercy you are able to do another human being a benefit or good turn, rejoice in the good which I do with you as my instrument, but do not rejoice in yourself. Do not flatter or please your own inclination, for in it lies hidden self-love. Turn your heart away from what was done and from yourself so that you never join together the two ideas, yourself and my benefit.

Never examine the gift itself, never rejoice in it or start analyzing what you feel or whether the feeling has come from me or from some other cause. That only separates you and me and delays your coming to me.Get quickly away from all these thoughts and try to unite yourself firmly to me. Avoid all the little tricks by which the mind provokes self-love for its own ability. Refer everything to me.

Don't glory in self or rejoice without me for any consolation or gift which you receive. Don't dally over the thing itself, where some self-love always lies lurking, but rejoice in me because I have shown my glory. Don't seek any praise for my gifts, and ascribe nothing to your own abilities. Live without following your own advice, judgment or opinion.

If you want to be my spouse, keep your heart chaste and pure, free and quite alienated from any other love but mine, and from being possessed by anything that I have made, so that it may be left entirely for me to dwell in. As soon as you detect any sensual love in your mind for any man, woman or any other creature whatsoever, sorrowfully lift up your heart to me and ask for the safe refuge of my grace and favour.

Examine all your actions, thoughts and desires, what is behind them, and, whether you are talking or silent, whether you are doing something or are resting, look closely into the innermost corners of your soul, into the very marrow of your thoughts and intentions, where you will often find that the root and seed of what you think is a divine growth is only human, impure and mere seeking to please your own appetite.

You will first come to know yourself by realizing your own disability and weakness. Whereas before, you thought you were something, now you will plainly find that you are nothing. If you work hard at looking into yourself every day and examining all your thoughts, you will realize your own weakness and imperfections. Then you will provoke sorrows for the sins you find in yourself and an earnest desire to get rid of them.

The labour and distress of finding your imperfections, and working to rid yourself of them, and the sorrow you feel, will be like a baptism for your soul. You can overcome everything by trusting in my mercy. Don't be faint-hearted. Trust in me and I shall make your crosses light, and I shall bear part of your burden.

29

Do not neglect the grace of God

Spend as much time as you can in good exercises which will help you to lift up your heart to me when you can't feel my grace powerfully at work in you. But never prefer your own pious devices to my inspirations. When you have learned to know my will – whether through the will of your superior, or by my providence – forsake your own inclinations.

When you feel a clear and straightforward inspiration from me inside you, obey me by leaving yourself and following me. I want you to forsake your own will, even in virtuous and praiseworthy things, so that you rely wholly on me, with firm and full confidence in me.

If you can't follow the prayers and pious exercises of other people, don't be discouraged or dejected. Don't respect people's pious exercises but their virtues. I distribute my gifts to people as they are constituted by nature, and according to the particular vocation to which I call each person. I give people things to do which are right for them and not for others, because people have different natures and different vocations. Even if you can't follow others' virtuous exercises, follow their virtues. You may be humble, merciful, patient, and resemble others in these virtues, even though you can't imitate them in the very same way of exercising those virtues. There is but one way to please me, which has always been one and the same for all my servants.

That is the way of charity or love, which is expressed in many different ways but has one and the same end; it is the way you must take by whatever means I decide are right for you. If you walk along the road of love by committing all things to me, and by humbling yourself under my mighty hand, and by seeking my glory in everything that you do or say, I shall never let you go astray, though you walk in the deepest darkness or ignorance, though you are vexed with great temptations and trials, and though you think you are quite forsaken and rejected by me.

Always think of your calling and do whatever agrees with it, being ready to do something else if you are directed to do so by my inspiration, providence and will. Do not measure your perfections by this or that person's account, or by your own judgment, but by my good pleasure, so that you do not try to reach this or that person's perfection, or the perfection that you yourself desire, but the perfection that I have decided is right for you.

Let the perfection you seek for be abundant or scarce as my will decides. Wish and pray that you may be the kind of person in my sight that my special will for you wants you to be.

30
Using the gifts of God for the good of others

I don't want you to neglect the gifts and graces I give you. But be careful not to raise yourself in my graces, by puffing yourself up with pride, boasting of them, glorying in them or wanting to please yourself with them. Use them all for my glory.

I don't like my gifts to come back to me fruitless, but with gain, as I warned everyone in my parable of the talents. Your eye in your body is not an eye only for itself, nor there for its own use and benefit, but so that it can help all your other organs to see. Any talents or gifts I have given you are not for your self alone, so that you reap their entire benefit, but are in you for the benefit of other members of my mystical body, so that with them you can help others, serve others, and help your neighbours to know my will and to do my commandments. I did not give them the things I gave you. In you I provided for them and for you. Similarly, for the same reason I have withheld many graces from you which I have given to others. When I gave things to others, I thought of you too, and gave them not for the sake of those others alone, but for you, because I gave them those graces for your benefit.

And so I want you to use my gifts to help other people as best you can. If you can do something they cannot, then the one charity in you all will make many of you with diverse gifts one body. Whatever this body has in one limb should be used to the benefit of the rest. Every member of my body ought to make one another a sharer in the gifts which every one of them receives, because of the union of the body and the communion of love which exists among them.

So be cheerful in serving your neighbours, glad to bear their burdens, meek to suffer with them, gentle to comfort them, ready to help them and willing to rejoice with them, so that no envy at all, no argument, no copying, no trying to please your own inclinations is found in you, or in your neighbours, but there is perfect love and communication of my gifts one with another, as between the members of one body. You have nothing that is your own. What do you possess that you have not received? You have nothing that is not mine. You have nothing that is given to you alone, that is, you have nothing that is given to you for yourself alone, but everything that you have received is committed to your care to be used entirely for the benefit of the whole body of my Church. Be careful with it, for I shall ask for an account of what you have done with it.

Never think that you are contented and perfectly

realized in being with me, but remember that if the physical or spiritual needs of your neighbours call you away from even profound contemplation, you must be ready to forsake your own consolation—the pleasures of devotion. Neglect your own pleasure and run in haste to help your neighbour for my sake. It is perfect love not to seek your own but your neighbour's good. That charity is more acceptable to me and more profitable to you than all the contemplation or devotion you practise on your own.

In addition, always remember that in all your actions, feelings, and things you choose or avoid, I must be your beginning, middle and end, so whatever you do or leave undone is for my sake. You are most acceptable to me when you leave yourself for my sake, because you forsake your own concerns and try to help your neighbours in their need. If you do anything for any other reason, whether for family bonds, or because of a specially close friendship, or for any gain or reward you expect, I shall reject it, however great or worthy the act may be in itself. The sacrifice must be offered for my sake.

31
Poverty of spirit

Do as many good works as possible with as much zeal and earnestness as possible. Hunger and thirst after justice and let no person seem to you weaker and more imperfect, more lacking in all virtues, and more unworthy of my grace, than yourself. Always keep your eyes on your own defects, and be sorry that you have so many imperfections and are without so many virtues. Remember that it is not your duty to look into other people's behaviour, their virtues, the ways they walk, and how they behave towards me.

I know what I have given everybody. I know too what account I want from each individual of what he or she has done. Imagine yourself in your own eyes to be the basest and wickedest of creatures and merely nothing. Be ashamed in my presence if you hear anyone praise you or offer a good opinion of you, and be sorry for it.

Be equally content to receive commendations or blame, and only think that you deserve to be blamed and do not deserve to be praised. As long as you complain and think that you have been injured, you are not purged of self-love. You should never take anything as an injury unless it is a wrong done to me.

32
The love of God

If you loved me perfectly, if you longed for me vehemently, you would think of nothing but how to come to me, and how to be united to me. You would always have such a hunger and thirst after justice that you would never be contented or satisfied with what you have done for the sake of my honour, however great the deeds, but would always be sorry that what you had done already was nothing at all.

Those who are inflamed with great love for any man or woman loathe food, drink and all other things which might otherwise delight them or be necessary to sustain their body. They pine away and grow sickly if they can't enjoy the person they love, or if they discover and realize that they are not loved in return. They languish just out of love and love alone. It makes them so that they can't take any joy in anything or find any peace unless they get the object of their love.

That is the way to love me, to find joy and consolation in me alone, and nothing but sorrow and affliction everywhere you do not find me. If you loved me as you ought to love me, you could not rest until you possessed me. A continual thirst, hunger and desire would burn in your soul, and you would not be allowed to enjoy any peace and quiet at all. I wish you languished with such a love towards me, or that you hated all other things and desired me alone.

If only you would show me your heart free from all other love, so that I might draw it to me and pierce it through and wound it utterly with my love. How happy you would be if, quite beside yourself and drunk with extreme love for me, you despised everything else, loathed all my creatures, and ran only after me, crying to me: 'I am wounded with your love'. You ought to be so inflamed with so fervent a love for me, that anyone who came near you would perceive nothing else about you but the heat of your love for me breathing out of you. Whoever talked to you should leave you edified and warmed with the flames of the love for me that he or she found burning in your soul.

If you want to love me, you must do so with your whole heart. I will not allow you to love me and to bring someone else into the relationship. In other words, you shouldn't love anything for any other reason than for my sake. You should love me purely, and that you can never do unless you love me for myself alone. I alone and no other reason must be why you love me. I am to be loved with infinite love and with a desire that knows no limit. Your soul should never allow its love for me to have any end or measure. Even if you think you love me infinitely, you should always want to love me more. My own love, you see, has no bounds. It is infinite and unlimited. It is never satisfied with itself and can never be satisfied and contented with the loving it does. Even if my love is immense, every day it goes on growing and increasing so that it is always bigger. True love always increases, and what is true love but good will?

A good will can't be restrained in any way. It is unending. Such is love. I know that you want to love me with your whole heart, as much as if all love there is were put together into one great enormous love. But that doesn't mean that you should want to love only in the sense that you can *only* love me if your love is really bigger than all other loves put together. The desire to love is good when it springs from pure and perfect charity, and when you desire me, love me, and want to grow in loving me, and to seek to love me as much alone as all loves together could possibly love me. Your desire to love shouldn't be like an appetite which is singled out because it is more important than all other apetites. It should spring forth because it is true love; and true love is so pure that it cannot be satisfied, and never can come to an end. Your love, if it's true love, should be so powerful that you believe, however much you love me, that your love for me is far, far less than the love you really want to show me, and that it never satisfies your desire to love me.

My love is not idle. My love does great things wherever it is. Where there is no real desire to do good, there certainly isn't any love. But don't get depressed if you find out that you just aren't doing good. As long as you want to, and you try to, your good will is as good and acceptable to me as if you had actually done all the good things you want to do. I shall never ask you to do what your nature can't do. It is not the quantity of good deeds but the power of love that delights me. Many people do good things which mean nothing to me, for they do them quite without love. What good to me is chaff without wheat? On the other hand, if you offer me the wheat of your love, also offer the chaff of your good works.

Though I am not interested in works without love, I shall look favourably on your love without works, if you are hindered by disability, necessity, obedience or any other lawful impediment which prevents you from doing good works. Then I shall accept your good will. But where you have the ability and the strength and the opportunity, if love persists, it grows and extends and comes towards me and, for my sake, towards your neighbour. I have put your neighbours with you in place of me, so that whatever you want to give me and cannot, you are able to give to them. So that you can do it all the more willingly, I have promised you that I will accept as readily from you, and reward in the same way, anything you have done towards your neighbours as if you had done it to me. If you are loving, then the effect will be that you love your neighbours for my sake, seeing me in them, serving me in them, helping me in them, bearing and suffering with me in them and, if they offend you, forgiving them for my sake.

There is nothing in any creature, and nothing forsaken for the love of me, that is so good that you will not find in me either things which are a hundred times better, purer, sweeter, pleasanter and more delightful than they were, whether it is beauty, sweetness, pleasantness, delight, love, truth, consolation, continual enjoyment of things that humans like, riches, glory, power and numerous other such things. All these things are in an infinite way more excellent and more perfect in me than in any creature whatsoever.

The smallest consolation from my goodness in your soul is greater than all the delights of the world and all the pleasures which any creature can afford. If things were measured justly, people would have to love me better than themselves or any other creature. But people leave me even though I am their greatest good. They despise my goodness. They forsake their true and only happiness and love themselves, delighting in the world from which all cares of the mind and all other troubles come.

Why are people deceived? If they delight in love, why don't they love me whose love is chaste, pure, holy and simple? I am essentially good in myself, being a pure good, and the chief and sovereign good, where the reward of love is unutterable delight and eternity. The love of the world breeds nothing in your soul but disquiet, bitterness, distraction, repentance and heaviness. Leave all worldly things and desire me alone. Unite yourself to me with all your soul, with all your heart, and with all your will. As long as you love creatures you will find what is in creatures – corrupt pleasures – and you will never be satisfied or contented.

Pray always to me that you may renounce the world and the love of my creatures, and be wholly converted to me and inwardly dedicated to me. Follow the inspiration of my grace and my advice, obey my exhortations and commit yourself to my providence. My inspiration always agrees with the Bible and with your obedience to your superiors.

Love is a great treasure and therefore I should be the place where it is kept. Where your treasure is, there is your heart also. If you want to know what you love, ask yourself what you most often think about, what you do with the greatest pleasure, most willingly listen to and desire most fervently, and what you seek most within yourself, for that is certainly your treasure, and in that treasure you will find the sweetest peace and greatest contentment. Yet people despise me and love corrupt, unclean and frail things which will soon decay, thrusting me clean out of human hearts, though I bought their salvation with my blood.

33
Praise of God

Always burn with a desire to praise, love, honour and please me from the bottom of your heart, by all the means you have, and as perfectly as I require from you. Revere, fear, love me for my sake so that you never allow yourself to displease or offend me.

Your heart should always be filled with a most faithful, fervent, and devout love of me, which should continually flow with strong currents every day closer and closer to me, and carry you with such great violence and run over so abundantly as to make you ready and desirous to do everything that may be to my glory. It should possess you so that you want to be quite free of all love, respect, desire or inclination towards yourself or any of my creatures, and to keep yourself in the same state – pure, clean, chaste for me alone, desiring me with a pure intention so that my will may be done in you, and there is no division between you and me, and you are closely joined to me, having renounced and forsaken all love of yourself and others.

Desire my will to be done in all things and in all men and women, and that everyone should know, love, honour, worship and serve me. You should rather suffer ten deaths than once consent to any sin.

Though it is highly unlikely that you can persist for long without committing a venial sin, you must not willingly yield to a venial sin, but be always resolved never to sin again.

I am so all-powerful that I stand in need of no praise, and no praise can make me more glorious than I am already. Nor can any creature praise and magnify me as I deserve. Though you must think yourself unworthy to praise me, you should desire to do so, so that the world may realize how all human praise is nothing in regard to my majesty, and how I am far greater than all the praise that may be given me, and how all creatures, when they have praised me as much as they can, have praised me far below the level at which I should be praised.

Vocal praise pleases me, and you must praise me thus with your voice whenever my Church commands you to say or sing anything. Yet that doesn't please me as much as the inward praise of the spirit. Profound contemplation and perfect knowledge of your own lowliness, weakness and the nothingness of yourself, is a sweet sacrifice to me and true praise of me. It will persuade you to humble yourself before me and all my creatures, and make you wish to be despised by them all for your inadequacies. The sorrow of a contrite heart is sweeter praise to me than a huge heap of many words and a tedious multitude of vocal prayers and nothing else.

You also praise me truly when you find me as acceptable when I send adversity as when I send prosperity, and when you thank me as much for the one as for the other. You also praise me greatly in shunning sin, seeking virtue, and thirsting for the honour of my name and glory. It is more pure than any vocal praise to keep your heart free from all vice, sloth, depression, contrariness and to unite yourself with me in peace, tranquillity and silence.

As soon as you feel any temptation, come to me and say: 'Lord, as soon as I feel this temptation, as soon as it enters my mind, I glorify you with all the praises of heaven to the honour and glory of your name'. If it is a very serious temptation, say: 'Most merciful God, though I am suffering a very troublesome temptation, I will endure it willingly for your sake alone, and if you wish me to suffer more serious temptations than this, I am ready to do so with all my heart'.

If you start thinking of beautiful, pleasurable or precious things, say: 'Sweet Lord, this comes from you who are most beautiful, good, sweet and desirable, because you are the greatest good. If you wish, I shall willingly forsake all your creatures. I shall willingly forsake all consolation, so that you alone may remain in my heart and wholly possess me'.

If you see a group of people or something very beautiful or a fine multitude, say to yourself: 'Most loving Lord, let a thousand thousand heavenly spirits praise you for me, and let ten thousand hundred thousand of those that stand before you praise your name for me, and let all the voices of your saints intercede to you for me, and let the beauty of every one of your creatures and the sweet harmony of them all glorify you for me for ever, world without end'.

34

Love and praise of God

If you want to love and praise me with all your heart, soul, strength, and ability, and wish to persevere in loving me until the end of your mortal life, you must exercise your love so that its flame is kept alive. Keep your mind free, apart, and without love of all I have made and all inward preoccupation with them, and separate from all the cares and troubles of this world, by lifting it up to me with a fervent desire to come to me, by desiring to love me vehemently, ardently, perfectly, faithfully and continually, and to do my will in all things.

You must always wish to see me who am most beautiful, to possess me who am most blessed, and to be with me who alone can grant you happiness, for I am the fountain of all happiness, sweetness and goodness. I am true happiness itself. Never separate yourself from me. Always have something in your mind which enables you to meditate on me, and which sparks love of me in you – some exercise which enables you to think of my sweetness and goodness and to praise my name. You can also meditate on something which makes you sorry for your weakness, inconstancy or ungratefulness, or make you pray for the dead and for the Church. Whatever you have to think about, think of it first with me, ask advice about it from me, and talk about it first to me, so that always, whether you are alone or with others, you talk to me and keep your heart lifted up to me, either by prayer or by praising my name.

Do whatever fits my honour, contents me or is my will. Do everything you can to ensure that my will is fulfilled in all my creatures. While your outward self is occupied with such external concerns, let your inward self remain with me, for you must never concern yourself so much with external things that your mind becomes distracted and runs wandering after this thought or that, and in that way all sorts of silly thoughts and vain fancies enter your soul.

When you have learned to do this, no external affairs will prevent you, especially if the exercise you are engaged in is a good and modest one, from the mental exercise of the love of me. You can speak to me, and be quietly united with me in your soul as well at that time as at any other, so long as you do not entangle your mind in thinking of vain and transitory things, or remain drowned in thoughts of the outward things you have to do in the world. As long as you want to keep your heart from the love of the things I have made, there is no person or thing that can win or take you away from me, even though you have an enormous number of things to do, so long as you do not imprint the images and pleasure of these things inwardly in your mind.

Never complain that external good works impede your loving me, or exercising your love towards me. Not they but your want of discretion, weakness and wrong inclinations hinder you, because they make you not only outwardly but inwardly busy thinking of my creatures. The more your mind is distracted the less it can remain recollected and peaceful within, let alone cleave to me. Nevertheless, don't be discouraged if sometimes human charity or obedience demand sometimes that you should be inwardly occupied and restless for my sake. I can quickly put right whatever you have disturbed for my sake so that afterwards you are all the closer to me.

Whatever does keep you from me, whether people, things, or your own wayward inclinations do not remain thus for long, for I am always ready to receive you again into my favour.

35
The transformation of a human being

If you want to be wholly with me, you have to forsake yourself entirely. You must submit yourself to extreme poverty and a lack of all worldly goods, if you are to obtain me who am the chief and greatest good. Do not be dismayed even if you are deprived of all human consolation, and you are without all human friendship, favour, and assistance.

Remember how a good soldier, in spite of friends, country, wife, children, the peace and goods of his home, forsakes them all and lives as a stranger in a foreign land, daily subjecting his life to dangerous work, painful journeys, continual watching, and various miseries, so that he may obtain riches and win honour. Similarly, you must forsake everything and become poor, and be without comfort and all my creatures, so that nothing is left in you that can give you peace but me alone. You must also banish the images of all things, and cleanse your mind of them all, and carry about the image of me alone, imprinted in your heart wherever you are and however you are, alone or in the company of others.

Whether you are eating or drinking, sleeping or waking, speaking or silent, you must always consider me a perfect pattern for imitation and direct the course of your life and transform yourself in accordance with the virtues and nature of my life. Whatever you eat should be eaten in the memory of my suffering. Whatever you drink should be the warm blood of my wounds breathing love into you. If you speak, look at me hearing your words and make sure you say nothing which is unseemly or may displease me. If you are silent, listen to me and search for my perfect will and pleasure. If you are asleep, rest on my heart, breathing my grace into your spirit and breathing out to me the precious treasure of your own heart.

Wherever you are, live in accordance with the pattern of my own life. Try to imitate my humility, affability, meekness, patience, chastity, piety, providence, compassion, and fervent, great and incomprehensible love. Imprint the image of these things in your soul, fill your mind with it, and banish from your thoughts all shapes and images of all other things whatsoever.

Behold the image of my humanity and passion until I raise you up to a higher level where you will be completely delivered from any impression or imagination, and are free from all exercises and actions, and remain peaceful and quiet, having entirely forsaken yourself.

In the meantime remember how I am always with you, and how I look into the hidden corners of your soul and the deepest secrets of your heart.

Learn to conceive how I am without any limits, and not circumscribed within any bounds. How I am eternal, unchangeable, unutterable and incomprehensible light. How I am worthy to be beloved. How I alone deserve to be desired. How I am wholly pure and sincere, without the least evil or smallest imperfection. Learn to conceive how I am wholly good, faithful and merciful, and ready always to reach out to human beings. Learn that I am a most constant and faithful lover, sweet comforter, mighty protector, and bountiful rewarder of all those who hope in me, and how I can give their souls more delight than all other things that can be desired. Let this perfect image of me wholly possess your mind and imprint it so deeply in it that you cannot allow yourself to meditate on anything else.

Stay united to me in inward solitariness, peace and tranquillity, waiting for me with great desire to follow me and submit to anything that I wish you to do or suffer. Renounce all love of yourself and all inclination to follow your own will.

Watch over yourself and examine your secret thoughts, and what moves and possesses you, and what you love – yourself, another creature, or me. If you find anything else in yourself, thrust it out. I shall never consent to share your love. I expect your whole love and I wish to rest in peace within you, alone. You must seek me to find me perfectly. If you want to enjoy me, banish all creatures from yourself, and allow no separation or impediment between yourself and me.

Rely on me and commit all your cares to me. Fix and settle your heart on me alone. See me only and no more than me in all things. I am in all and all in all, and wait patiently with long-suffering until you find me. Be content to wait for me again and again and never be weary of waiting until you find me, relying on my goodness and on my most wise providence, which is full of love for you. When I don't turn up, expect me patiently, for I will come at the last without any doubt. Be free from all your own desires, and separate yourself from all love for and delight in worldly things. Divide yourself from all fancy and imagination, and cleave to me utterly in simplicity and nakedness of heart.

Conclusion

I decided to have my written exhortations laid before
your eyes, because you are quite pleased when you get
letters and messages from your friends which do no
more than distract your heart, troubling it often in an
odd way. Instead I have given you these worthwhile
messages, so that your mind may lead you to love me. I
want you to observe the precepts and take the advice I
have put before you, so that your spiritual heart may
be delighted. I have not tried to pleasure your ears
with fine phrases and trumpery words, but to feed
your loving soul with truth and wholesome advice. All
that remains now is is to warn you to be watchful and
diligent, for I stand knocking at the very door of your
heart. So open your heart to me. Give me your heart
and desire me alone, seeing that I desire you so much.
Rest assured of this one thing: you can never receive
me as long as you love anything besides me. You can
never have me as long as you possess yourself. So leave
yourself and forsake your own self, so that I alone may
possess you, and you alone may possess me. The time
of this world is meagre, but the world to come has time
and to spare: it is eternal; it has no end.

Be watchful. Receive me as your husband—my
soul, my daughter, my spouse. Love me, your
Redeemer and your Lord, and think always of me.
Cleave to me and persevere with me to the end. Live
happily in me from now on. Farewell.

HYMN

by Philip Howard
(died in the Tower of London, 1595)

O, Christ, the glorious Crown
Of virgins that are pure;
Who dost a love and thirst for Thee
Within their minds procure;
Thou art the spouse of those
That chaste and humble be,
The hope, the life, the only help
Of such as trust in Thee.

All charity of those
Whose souls Thy love doth warm;
All simple pleasures of such minds
As think no kind of harm;
All sweet delights wherewith
The patient hearts abound,
Do blaze Thy name, and with Thy praise
They make the world resound.

The sky, the land, the sea,
And all on earth below,
The glory of Thy worthy Name
Do with their praises show.

A letter from Jesus Christ

The winter yields Thee praise,
And summer doth the same,
The sun, the moon, the stars and all
Do magnify Thy name.

The roses that appear
So fair in outward sight;
The violets which with their scent
Do yield so great delight;
The pearls, the precious stones,
The birds, Thy praise do sing,
The woods, the wells, and all delights,
Which from this earth do spring.

What creature, O sweet Lord,
From praising Thee can stay?
What earthly thing but, filled with joy,
Thine honour doth bewray?
Let us, therefore, with praise
Thy mighty works express,
With heart and hand, with mind, and all
Which we from Thee possess.